GOOCHLAND COUNTY [VIRGINIA] ROAD ORDERS

1728-1744

Virginia Genealogical Society
Richmond, Virginia

Published With Permission from the

Virginia Transportation Research Council
(A Cooperative Organization Sponsored Jointly by the Virginia
Department of Transportation and
the University of Virginia)

HERITAGE BOOKS
2008

HERITAGE BOOKS
AN IMPRINT OF HERITAGE BOOKS, INC.

Books, CDs, and more—Worldwide

For our listing of thousands of titles see our website
at
www.HeritageBooks.com

Published 2008 by
HERITAGE BOOKS, INC.
Publishing Division
100 Railroad Avenue #104
Westminster, Maryland 21157

Copyright © 2002 Virginia Genealogical Society

All rights reserved. No part of this book may be reproduced or transmitted in any form or by any means, electronic or mechanical, including photocopying, recording or by any information storage and retrieval system without written permission from the author, except for the inclusion of brief quotations in a review.

International Standard Book Number: 978-0-7884-3663-5

GOOCHLAND COUNTY ROAD ORDERS 1728-1744

by

Nathaniel Mason Pawlett
Faculty Research Historian

Virginia Highway & Transportation Research Council
(A Cooperative Organization Sponsored Jointly by the Virginia Department of Highways &
Transportation and the University of Virginia)

Charlottesville, Virginia

June 1975
Revised March 2004
VHTRC 75-R71

PREFACE

The Virginia Highway and Transportation Research Council is a cooperative organisation sponsored jointly by the Virginia Department of Highways and Transportation and the University of Virginia and is located on the Grounds of the University at Charlottesville. The Council engages in a comprehensive program of research in the field of transportation. As a part of its program the Council, in December 1972, began research on the history of road and bridge building technology in Virginia. The initial effort was concerned with truss bridges; a complementary effort concentrating on roads got underway in October 1973.

The evolution of the road system of Virginia is in many ways inseparable from the social, political and technological developments that form the history of the Commonwealth. Despite this, there are few extant serious works on the history of roads in Virginia. Those which have been produced focus on internal improvements and turnpike development before the War Between the States. Little has been done on the period from Reconstruction through the creation of the system of state highways in the earlier part of this century.

Accordingly, it was decided to investigate the development of the roads of Albemarle County during the period 1725-1925 as a pilot project, and to use this experience to produce a "History of Albemarle County Roads" and a procedural handbook for the writing of Road Histories. During the early stages of this project it was necessary to examine and extract all the Road Orders for the Counties from which Albemarle was formed as well as the Orders for Albemarle when it, still contained the Counties of Amherst, Buckingham, Fluvanna, Nelson, and a part of Appomattox. The Road Orders concerning Albemarle will ultimately be published with the Road History but the broad applicability of those for Goochland, Louisa and early Albemarle, and the opinions of various authorities throughout the state who have examined them, indicate that they should have separate publication in order to make them generally available to individual scholars through libraries and educational institutions. Therefore, this publication has been prepared.

GOOCHLAND COUNTY ROAD ORDERS 1728-1744

By

Nathaniel Mason Pawlett
Faculty Research Historian

INTRODUCTION

The roads are under the government of the county courts, subject to be controuled by the general court. They order new roads to be opened whenever they think them necessary. The inhabitants of the county are by them laid off into precincts, to each of which they allot a convenient portion of the public roads to be kept in repair. Such bridges as may be built without the assistance of artificers, they are to build. If the stream be such as to require a bridge of regular workmanship, the court employs workmen to build it, at the expence of the whole county. If it be too great for the county, application is made to the general assembly, who authorize individuals to build it, and to take a fixed toll from all passengers, or give sanction to such other proposition as to them appears reasonable.

Thomas Jefferson, *Notes on the State of Virginia*, 1781.

The establishment and maintenance of public roads was an important function of the County Court during the colonial period in Virginia. Each road was opened and maintained by an Overseer or Surveyor of the Roads charged with this responsibility and appointed by the Gentlemen Justices. He was usually assigned all the "Labouring Male Titheables" living on or near the road for this purpose.

Major projects, such as bridges over rivers, demanding considerable expenditures were executed by Commissioners appointed by the Court to select the site and contract with workmen for the construction. Where bridges connected two counties, a commission was appointed by each and they cooperated in executing the work.

The Road Orders contained in the Goochland County Court Order Books covering the period 1728-1744 are the principal extant evidence concerning the early roads of the County. During this period Goochland stretched southward to the Appomattox River and west to the "Ledge", or Blue Ridge, and contained all or parts of the present Counties of Albemarle, Amherst, Appomattox, Bedford, Buckingham, Campbell, Cumberland, Fluvanna, Nelson and Powhatan.

Insofar as possible, all the Orders were extracted verbatim and the capitalisation, spelling and punctuation have been reproduced without any attempt at correction or consistency.

Persons desiring more specific information may consult the *Goochland County Historical Society Magazine*. Beginning with the Spring 1975 issue (Volume 7, Number 1), these Road Orders appear there, with comprehensive annotation by Mr. Elie Weeks.

THE DEVELOPMENT OF GOOCHLAND COUNTY

Note: As originally published in paper format, this volume included maps showing the evolution of the county. Maps are not included in the revised/electronic version due to legibility and file size considerations. Instead, a verbal description is provided.

As created in 1728 from the western reaches of Henrico County, Goochland stretched from the present-day eastern borders of Goochland and Powhatan counties westward to the Blue Ridge Mountains. In its original form, Goochland contained the modern counties of Goochland, Powhatan, Cumberland, Fluvanna, Buckingham, Nelson, and Amherst, in their entireties. In addition, the northern sections of Appomattox, Campbell, and Bedford, and the southern two-thirds of Albemarle County were also within Goochland's original boundaries.

The creation of Albemarle County in 1744 and Cumberland County in 1749 removed most of Goochland's southern and western territory, reducing it to its modern size and boundaries.

Order Book 1, Goochland County

18 June 1728 Old Style, p. 9
Ferry to be kept [Italicized entries are marginal notes in original text]
William Mayo and Allen Howard Gent. are appointed to agree with Sarah Atkinson for keeping ffery one year of a Court day to set over foot people only to Court./.

18 June 1728 Old Style, p. 9
Surveyors of the road
Following Surveyors of the roads are appointed Viz^t. William Womack from Tuckahoe Creek to Stony Creek, George Payne from Stony Creek to Beverdam Creek, John Webb from Beverdam Creek to Treasurer's Runn Lilliard Ballew from thence to the Byrd, Joseph Thomas from the Byrd to Patricks fford, James Nowlin ffrom, the river road up the Back road to the Bridge over Beverdam Creek below Major Bollings Mill, John Mackbride from Bridge of the Said Back road untill it meets the river road, Tarlton ffleming Gent. from the County Line to fine Creek, John Quin from fine Creek to Solomons Creek, John Saunders from Solomons Creek to Deep Creek, George Stoveall from Deep Creek to Muddy Creek Mathew Cox from Muddy Creek to Willis's Creek and it is ordered that George Stoveall and Mathew Cox with the Several Titheables in each of their precincts do meet at Muddy Creek to repair bridge over the Same as often as there Shall be occasion Nathaniel Basset of the road from John fford's to Ward's appamatox ridge, Stephen Chastain of the River road from the County Line on the South Side James River to the Pit./.

20 August 1728 Old Style
Surveyor of the road
Anthony Hoggat is appointed Surveyor of the back road over Tuckahoe Creek from the County line upwards./.

17 Sept. 1728 Old Style, p. 25
Surveyor of the road
Nicholas Cox is appointed Surveyor of the road from Richard Parker's on letalone Creek the best way down to the Manakin Town road and it is ordered that the Inhabitants near the said road be exempt from clearing any other roads./.

17 Sept. 1728 Old Style, p. 25
Surveyor of the road
William Womack is appointed Surveyor of the road from Tuckahoe Bridge to Woodson's mill Creek./.

18 Sept. 1728 Old Style, p. 31
Surveyor of the road
Ordered that a convenient road be cleared from the Ferry landing through the low ground of Jacob Micheaux for the upper and lower Inhabitants on the South Side James River John Quin is appointed Surveyor thereof./.

19 Nov. 1728 Old Style, p. 49
Surveyor appointed
Allin Howard Gent. is appointed Surveyor of the road from the Court house into the Back road above Major Bolling's mill. Henry Wood is appointed Surveyor of the road from Tuckahoe Creek mill to Manakin Town Ferry Stephen Hughes is appointed Surveyor of the road from the Court house Ferry down the South side of the James River the most convenient way for the lower Inhabitants to come to Court, and it is ordered-that the Inhabitants between the main road and the River clear this said road./.

21 Jan. 1728, O.S., p. 64
Surveyor of the road
Ordered that the Titheables of James Moss, David Clarkson, Thomas Golsby, George Thompson, Samuel Butler, Andrew Pruit, do assist in clearing road from Tuckahoe mill to ffery over James River at the Manakin Town./.

21 Jan. 1728, O.S. p. 64
Surveyor of the road
Ordered that the road from John ffords towards Appamatox ridge be continued over both the branches of ffine Creek, Nathaniel Basset is appointed Surveyor thereof./.

18 Feb. 1728, O.S. p. 73
Surveyor of the road
Jacob Micheaux is appointed Surveyor of the road from fine Creek to Solomons Creek, and from the ffery to the main road upwards./.

19 March 1728, O.S. p. 83
Ferry appoint'd
Sarah Atkinson is permitted to keep ffery and the rate of fferriage for a man is Settled at 3P and for a Horse at 3P. William Mayo Daniel Stoner Gent. are desired to agree with her for keeping a County fferry./.

19 March 1728, O.S. p. 83
Surveyor of the road
David Walker is appointed Surveyor of the road from the Courthouse into the back road above Major Bolling's Mill./.

20 May 1729, O.S. p. 97
Surveyor of the road
Constant Perkins is appointed Surveyor of the road from Thomas Murrel's to the back road. Anthony Hoggat from Tuckahoe Creek mill towards Hanover County as far as the County line./.

20 May 1729, O.S. p. 97
fferry app^d.
Stephen Hughes on the behalf of Sarah Atkinson agrees to keep fferry at the Court house for 800 Ibs. of tobacco p Annum and to let over all persons living in the County on Court days and all other publick days and the Sherif and his Officers at all times./.

20 May 1729, O.S. p. 97
Surveyor of the Road
Warham Easly is appointed Surveyor of the road from Richard Parker's on Letalone Creek the best way down to the Manakin Town road and it is ordered that the Inhabitants near the said road be exempt from clearing any other road./.

19 August 1729, O.S. p. 143
Surveyor of the road
David Walker is appointed Surveyor of the Road from the Court house into the back road above Major Bolling's mill and it is ordered that severall male labouring titheables of Josepn Woodson, Henry Adkins William May, Richard Cocke, William Moor, Edward Curd, Abraham Perkins, and John Moor do assist in Clearing the said road./.

16 Sept. 1729, O.S. p. 146
Surveyor of the Road.
Stephen Chastain is appointed Surveyor of the Road from ffine Creek to the County line below the lower Manakin Creek./.

16 Sept. 1729, O.S. p. 148
Surveyor of the road.
Henry Wood is appointed Surveyor of the Road from Tuckahoe Creek mill to the main river road, and it is ordered that the severall male labouring Titheables of Thomas Wadlow, Joseph Watkins, Thomas Joplin, James Moss, David Clarkson, Thomas Golsby, George Thompson, Samuell Butler, Andrew Pruit, John Sorrell, Mathew Collins, George Perrin, Robert Burton, and Henry Wood do assist in clearing the same./.

21 Oct. 1729, O.S. p. 175
Tuckahoe bridge to be built
John Woodson and Allin Howard Gent. are appointed to meet Richard Randolph and Joseph Mayo Gent. on Saturday the eight day of November next at Tuckahoe Bridge to treat with workmen about rebuilding the same./.

21 Oct. 1729, O.S. p. 175
Surveyor of the road.
Philip Thomas is appointed Surveyor of the road from Richard Parker's on let alone Creek the best way down to the Manakin Town road, and it is ordered that the titheables dwelling on the South side of the said road do clear the same./.

16 Dec. 1729, O.S. p. 187
Surveyor of the Road.
On the motion of Henry Cary Gent. leave is granted him to Clear a road from Buckingham downwards the most convenient way Edward Wood is appointed Surveyor thereof./.

17 Dec. 1729, O.S. p. 191
fferry appointed
On the motion of Dudley Digges Gent. leave is granted him to keep a fferry from the point of the ffork of James River to both sides of the River and from each side to the point of ffork the rate of fferriage 2 pence for man and 2 pence for horse./.

17 Dec. 1729, O.S. p. 191
Surveyor of the Road.
Ordered that a Road be cleared from the fferry landing from the South Side of the James River opposite to the point of ffork in such manner as to pass by a Gravelly Fall of Willis's Creek by 3/4 of a mile below a plantation belonging to William Mayo Gent. and from thence the best way the ground will admit to the main Road, and from fferry landing on the North side of James River opposite to the point of ffork the best way the ground will admit to that River Road James Nevill is appointed surveyor of both said Roads. Ordered that the titheables inhabiting on the South side of James River above Willis's Creek do clear that part of the Road lying between the said Creek and the fferry landing and that the titheables of Benjamin Harrison Gent. do clear the other part of the Road lying below the said Creek./

17 Feb. 1729, O.S. p. 213
Surveyor of the Road.
John Prior is appointed Surveyor of the Road from lower Beverdam Bridge to little licking hole Creek./.

17 Feb. 1729, O.S. p. 220
Bever dam Bridge.
Ordered that the Bridge over Bever dam Creek below Bolling's Mill be kept in repair by the titheables who clear the Road below the said Bridge./.

17 March 1729, O.S. p. 221
Surveyor of the Roads.
On the motion of Ebenezer Adams on behalf of himself and others it is ordered that a road be cleared from Bever dam Bridge near John Prior's to pass by John Wright's Plantation cross Wild Boar swamp near Elk lick by William Owen's Plantation cross the North Branch of the Bird to Elk ford on the Bird to end at Martin King's. John Prior is appointed Surveyor of the said road from Bever dam Bridge to John Rights; John Laine from John Rights to Great Licking hole, Martin Dunken from Great Licking hole to the South branch of the Bird, John Bostick from the South branch of the Bird to Elk ford, Martin King from Elk ford to the River./.

19 May 1730, O.S.
fferry to be kept.
Ordered that George Payne and William Cabbell Gent. treat with Stephen Hughes about keeping the fferry at the Court house and that they report their proceedings therein to the next Court./.

Order Book 2, Goochland County
First page is torn. Exact date cannot be determined on second page

July Court 1730. O.S. p. 2
Surveyor of the Road.
On the Petition of Marmaduke Hix it is Ordered that a Road be cleared from the upper branch of ffine Creek across the fork of Deep Creek thence up the ridge between Deep Creek and Muddy Creek and that at the several male labouring titheables living [page torn] between no other two Roads do assist in clearing the same. Marmaduke Hix is appointed Surveyor thereof./.

July Court, 1730, p. 3
Surveyor of the Road.
Nicholas Cox is appointed Surveyor of the River Road on the South side of James River from, Deep Creek to Muddy Creek in the room of George Stoveall./.

15 Sept. 1730, O.S. p. 27
Randolph permitted to clear road.
On the motion of Isham Randolph leave is granted him to clear a road from his Plantation above Treasurer's Runn into the main Road along a ridge of land passing by the Plantation of Joseph Jackson.

17 Nov. 1730, O.S. p. 51
Stephen Hughes undertakes to keep a fferry at the Plantation where Widow Atkinson lately dwelt and to set over on all Court days all persons who live in the County and the Sherif and his Officers at all times. In Consideration of which service it is the opinion of the Court that there be levied for the said Stephen annually 1600 lbs. of tobacco with Cask and conveinency, and that the said Stephen be excused from listing one titheable./.

16 Feb. 1730, O.S. p. 68
Jones Creek bridge to built
Edward Scot undertakes to build a good strong and Substantial over Jones's Creek to fit for Carts to pass and to keep the same in repair for the Space of Seven years after the Same is finished and at the expiration of the said Term to leave the Said bridge in, good and sufficient repair for which it is considered by the Court that there by levy'd for the said Edward Scot and in his name at the laying on of the next county levy 4,000 lbs. of tobacco with Cask

and with Cask and Conveniency provided said bridge to then finish and that the said Edward Scot then or at any Court before enter in Bond with good and sufficient Security to comply with the agreement before said on his part made.

16 Feb. 1730, O.S. p. 68
Bever dam Creek bridge to be built--
Edward Scot undertakes to build a good Strong and Substantial bridge over Bever dam Creek fit for Carts to pass and to keep the same in repair for the Space of Seven years after the same is finished and after the expiration of the Said Term to leave the Said bridge in good and Sufficient repair for which it is considered by the Court that there be levyd for the said Edward Scot a [page torn] laying on of the next County levy five thousand [page torn] with Cask Conveniency Provided the [page torn] finished and that the said Edward Scot then or at [page torn] enter into bond with good and Sufficient Security for [page torn] the agreement aforesaid on his part made

16 Feb. 1730, O.S. p. 68
Surveyor of the road
Edward Scot is appointed Surveyor of all the roads between [page torn] in this County and of the road passing through the Manacantonroad.

16 Feb. 1730, O.S. p. 69
Surveyor of the road
Ordered that the severall Male labouring titheables in the Precincts whereof James Nowlin and David Walker are appointed Surveyors do jointly assist in repairing the bridge over Beverdam Creek on the middle road

16 Feb. 1730, p. 79
Surveyor of the Road
Ordered that the titheables of William Chamberlaine under the care of William May, Charles Spurlock and John Richardson and their titheables do assist John Mc.Bird in Clearing the road of which he is appointed Surveyor

16 Feb. 1730, O.S. p. 79
Surveyor of the road--
On the Motion of Henry Wood who was formerly appointed Surveyor of the road from Tuckahoe Creek mill into the river road towards the Church and fferry, it is Ordered that he do clear the said Road such way as he shall judge most convenient so as that the same do not prejudice any person's Plantation by passing through it

17 March, 1730 O.S., p. 88
Manacanton Road
On the motion of Edward Scot for leave to alter the road which passes through the Manacanton low grounds it is Ordered that Glaude Gore and Gideon Chambon be Summoned to appear at the next Court to make their objections thereto

18 May 1731, O.S. p. 105
Survr of road
Thomas Turpin is appointed Surveyor of the Road from the ffork of the Road between Jones's Creek and fine Creek so far as to extend over the long branch and it is ordered that all the titheables adjacent to the said Road so far up the same as to include the titheables of William Easly and James Cock to assist in Clearing it

18 May 1731, O.S. p. 105
Surveyor [page torn]
[page torn]asse appointed Surveyor of the Road from the long branch [page torn] between Jones's Creek and fine creek upwards as farr as cross the ffork ffine Creek including the upper Creek with a Slash on the upper Side

18 May 1731, O.S. p. 106
Surveyor of the road
Anthony Hughes is appointed Surveyor of the road from the Slash on the upper side of the upper branch of ffine Creek to the Chappell and it is ordered that the Titheables of Joel Chandler William Chandler Bartholomew Stovall and William Davis and all others within that neighbourhood do assist in clearing the said road

18 May 1731, O.S., p. 106
Surveyor of the road
John Franklin is appointed Surveyor of the road from ffine Creek to Solomons Creek and it is Ordered that the titheables of Daniel Stoner Daniel Johnson, John Cox, ffrederick Cox, Joseph John Isaac Hughes Nicholas Wilkinson and all others within that neighbourhood do assist in clearing the said roads

18 May 1731, O.S., p. 108
Dickins to clear a road--
On the motion of Thomas Dickins leave is granted him to clear a road from his dwelling house to the main road provided the same not pass through a person's clear ground

18 May 1731, O.S., p. 108
Surveyor of road
Jacob Micheaux is appointed Surveyor of the road from the fork of the fferry road upwards into the main road and it is Ordered that

the titheables of John Wood, Samuell Spencer D[page torn] Anthony Morgan and Paul Micheaux and of such other persons as inhabit within that neighbourhood do assist in clearing the same

18 May 1731, O.S., p. 117
Surveyor of the road--
Joseph Woodson is appointed Surveyor of the Road from the Courthouse to the fferry Landing, and it is Ordered that John Webb, John M^c.brid and David Walker, who are Surveyors of the roads adjacent and the titheables in the Severall precincts do assist in clearing the said road and that each Surveyor warn his own Gang to appear according to the appointment of Joseph Woodson aforesaid

18 May 1731, O.S. p. 124
Manacanton road--
Claude Gorey and Gideon Chambon appear and their objections against altering Manacanton road being considered it is Ordered that the road passing along the River Side in the Manacanton be kept open untill the new Church be built in King William Parish and that then the said road be Stopd and a new one cleared from the ferry landing to the back road on the hills to pass between the Land of Gideon Chambon and Claude Gorey of which Edward Scot is appointed Surveyor

15 June 1731, O.S. p. 127
Surveyor of road--
Stephen Cox is appointed Surveyor of the road from the fferry into the main road & leave is granted him to turn the said road. Benjamin Allen Thomas Lawhan, John Lewis Stephen Woodson, Josiah Woodson & that titheables will clear the said road & also a bridle way from the fferry to the Church.

15 June 1731, O.S. p. 127
Surveyor of road--
Daniell Hix is appointed Surveyor of the road from Buck branch to the County bridge the titheables of Thomas Randolph deceased are ordered to clear the Same.

15 June 1731, O.S. p. 127
Surveyor of road
William Womack is appointed Surveyor of the road from Buck branch to the Mill & the titheables adjacent thereto are to assist in clearing the Same.

15 June 1731, O.S. p. 127
Surveyor of road
George Raine is appointed Surveyor of the road from genitoe Creek on the back road into Hoggats road the titheables under George Payne Henry Wood & Anthony Hoggat are to assist in clearing the said road.

17 Aug. 1731, O.S. p. 175
Surveyor of road.
James Spears is appointed Surveyor of the road from the widow Blackburn's to the County line./.

17 Aug. 1731, O.S. p. 189
Surveyors.
The Surveyors of the roads are continued./.

21 Sept. 1731, O.S. p. 195
Surveyor of the road
Ordered that Thomas Dickin's titheables at Long Acre be added to James Spears Surveyor of the road./.

Order Book 3, Goochland County

17 Nov. 1731, O.S. p. 16
Surveyors of roads appointed.
John Dunn is appointed Surveyor of the road in the room of Constant Perkins, Richard Wade is appointed Surveyor from the upper Tuckahoe bridge to the County line, Joseph Watkins is appointed Surveyor from Tuckahoe mill to the River road in the room of Henry Wood, Joseph ffarrar is appointed Surveyor from Tuckahoe mill to Hanover line, And Richard Wade, Anthony Hoggat, Joseph ffarrar, and their Gangs are to assist in repairing the bridge on Tuckahoe near Hardings./.

17 Nov. 1731, O.S. p. 16
ffleming to clear road.
On the motion of John ffleming Gent. leave is granted him to open the old road called Stephens road./.

17 Nov. 1731, O.S. p. 16
Holman to clear road.
On the motion of James Holman Gent. leave is granted him to clear a road from his dwelling house into the main road./.

17 Nov. 1731, O.S. p. 16
Cabbell to clear road.
On the motion of William Cabbell Gent. leave is granted him to clear a road from his dwelling house into the main road./.

21 Dec. 1731, O.S. p. 21
Surveyors of the roads.
On the motion of Allen Howard Gent. Ordered that a road be cleared from the Bird Creek to the North branch of James River at Mount Misery fford and that Samuel Birks be Surveyor thereof, from thence to Rock fish River the best way the grounds will permit, Patrick Mullin is appointed Surveyor as far as opposite to Mr. Richard Cocke's Plantation where John Ripley is Overseer, John Ripley Surveyor from thence as far as opposite to Mr. Edward Scott's Plantation where John Tuly is Overseer, and John Tuly Surveyor from thence to Rock Fish River./.

21 Dec. 1731, O.S. p. 21
road to be viewed
On the Petition of Nicholas Cox it is Ordered that William Mayo Gent. do view the ground through which he petitions for a road and make report thereof to the next Court./.

21 Dec. 1731, O.S. p. 21
Surveyor of the road.
Stephen Hughes is appointed Surveyor of the road from the Court house to the fferry landing and the Gangs formerly appointed to assist Joseph Woodson about the said road are to work on the same./.

21 Dec. 1731, O.S., p. 34
Surveyor of Road.
On the petition of Stephen Woodson praying leave to alter the road from the Manakin town fferry to the main road on the North side of James River John Woodson and Allen Howard, Gent. are appointed to view the ground and to direct the most convenient way for making the said road Stephen Cox is appointed Surveyor thereof and the titheables formerly assigned him are to clear the same./.

15 Feb. 1731 O.S., p. 38
road to be viewed.
Daniel Stoner Gent. is appointed in the room of William Mayo Gent. to view the ground through which Nicholas Cox petitions for a road and to report the same to the next Court./.

20 March 1731 O.S., p. 40
Titheables for Parker's road.
Ordered that the following titheables be added to the precinct of which Richard Parker is Surveyor beginning at the place where Philip Thomas leaves off and from thence to the lower fork of Little Guinea (Viz^t.) Samuel White, William Wheeler, Thomas Boesand, the Titheables of ffrances Epes, of Henry Anderson, William M^c.Coy, John Edmunds, Timothy Lee, Hutchins Burton, Young Stokes, James Code, David Hattaway, John Bostick, James Thompson./.

20 March 1731 O.S., p. 46
Cox order for a road.
Daniel Stoner Gent. reports that the road which Nicholas Cox uses through the land of John Woodson Gent. is not prejudicial to the said Woodson and it is ordered to be continued./.

16 May 1732 O.S., p. 66
Grand Jury's Presentments.
...Stephen Hughes for not keeping the road from ffine Creek to the fferry landing in repair...

16 May 1732 O.S., p. 66
Grand Jury's Presentments.
Stephen Cox for not keeping the fferry landing in repair...

16 May 1732 O.S., p. 66
Grand Jury's Presentments.
Surveyor of the road from the Court house to the fferry landing for not keeping it in repair...

Grand Jury's Presentments.
...Surveyor of the road from Bever dam bridge to Dover mill for not keeping it in repair...

16 May 1732 O.S., p. 68
Bridge to be built.
On a motion for a bridge to be built over Deep Creek it is the opinion of the Court that the same is necessary and that workmen be agreed with at the next Court in the meantime John Woodson and Daniel Stoner Gent. are appointed to view the most convenient place for erecting the same./.

16 May 1732 O.S., p. 69
Moseby to turn road.
On the motion of Richard Moseby leave is granted him to turn the road near his Plantation./.

18 July 1732 O.S., p. 89
Hogatt & c. to view road at Manakin tow^n.
Anthony Hoggatt and Stephen Hughes are appointed to view the Manakin town roads and to report their Opinion which is most proper to be kept open or if another may be more conveniently made to supply the use of these roads./.

15 Aug. 1732 O.S., p. 95
Road to be cleared.
On the Petition of Thomas Saunders it is ordered that a road be cleared from Thomas Murrell's towards the head of Licking hole Creek and Thomas Saunders is appointed Surveyor thereof./.

15 Aug. 1732 O.S., p. 102
Road to be altered.
Ordered that the Surveyor alter the road over Deep Creek if he think it necessary and that the titheables who clear the road above and below the said Creek do join in making a bridge over the same./.

15 Aug. 1732 O.S., p. 109
Stoner & c. to view road at Manacan town.
Daniel Stoner, Tarlton ffleming, and Thomas Dickins are appointed to view the Manacan town roads and to report their Opinion which is most proper to be kept open or if another may be more conveniently made to supply the use of those roads./.

19 September 1732 O.S., p. 111
Surveyor of the Road.
John Harris is appointed Surveyor of the road from ffine Creek to Jones's Creek./.

19 Sept. 1732 O.S., p. 113
Manacan town road to be cleared
Ordered that a road be cleared from Claude Gorey's into the road going to the bridge over Jones's Creek according to a Plan thereof drawn by William Mayo Gent. and that the River road which passes through Anthony Bennins land be stopped./.

19 Sept. 1732 O.S., p. 113
Surveyor of the Road.
Philip Webber is appointed Surveyor of the road from Dover mill to Beaver dam Bridge./.

19 Sept. 1732 O.S., p. 114
Surveyor of the Road.
Ordered that a road be cleared from about two miles above The mouth of the Bird Creek up the Country as far as Buck Island Joseph Barringer is appointed Surveyor of the said road./.

19 Sept. 1732 O.S., p. 115
Surveyor of the road.
David Davis is appointed Surveyor of the road in the room of Martin Dunkin and it is ordered that he turn the said road such way as will be most convenient./.

7 Oct. 1732 O.S., p. 124
Deep Creek road to be viewed.
Daniell Stoner Gent. is appointed to view the road over Deep Creek & to report the most convenient way to carry the same./.

16 Jan. 1732 O.S., p. 127
Surveyors of the roads.
Jacob Winfrey is appointed Surveyor of the road in the room of Marmaduke Hix, Benjamin Moseby is appointed Surveyor of the road in the room of Nicholas Cox, William Allen is appointed Surveyor of the road in the room of Nathaniel Bassett, Edmund Butler is appointed Surveyor of the road in the room of James Spears./.

20 March 1732 O.S., p. 133
Surveyor of the road.
John Cox is appointed Surveyor of the Road in the room of John ffranklin./.

20 March 1732 O.S., p. 134
Surv^r. of the road.
Thomas Applebury is appointed Surveyor of the road in the room of Patrick Mullin./.

20 March 1732 O.S., p. 137
Grand Jury vs. Hughes.
On the Presentment of the Grand Jury against Stephen Hughes for not keeping the road in repair the said Stephen appears and making no legal objection it is ordered that he be fined 15 shillings Curr^t. money./.

20 March 1732 O.S., p. 137
Surv^r. of road.
ffrancis James is appointed Surveyor of the road in the room of Stephen Hughes./.

22 March 1732 O.S., p. 166
Surveyor of the Road.
Thomas Cawthorn is appointed Surveyor of the road in the room of Samuell Burk./.

15 May 1733 O.S., p. 178
Randolph to clear a road.
On the motion of William Randolph Junr. leave is granted him to clear a road from opposite his landing into the main Manacan town Road./.

15 May 1733 O.S., p. 178
Surveyor of the road.
Samuell Burk is appointed Surveyor of the road from Joseph Barringer's to Buck Island./.

15 May 1733 O.S., p. 180
Howard & c. to view Bridges
Allin Howard, James Skelton, Anthony Hoggatt, & Henry Wood, are appointed to view the Bridges over the two Tuckahoe Creeks and to report to the next Court whether they can be mended by the Surveyors of the roads./.

19 June 1733 O.S., p. 197
Road to be cleared.
Ordered that a road be cleared from the Mountains down the ridge between the North River & Pamunkey River the most convenient way Robert Adams is appointed Surveyor thereof and the adjacent inhabitants to clear it./.

19 June 1733 O.S., p. 199
Road to be cleared.
Ordered that Jacob Winfrey do cause the road to be worked that he is Surveyor of as far as Horn quarter Horse penn, and a bridle way to be cleared./.

18 Sept. 1733 O.S., p. 210
Road to be cleared.
Ordered that the road be cleared from near Richard Parker's to the upper inhabitants on Appamattox River, Joseph Morton, Junr. is appointed Surveyor thereof and the titheables inhabiting between M^r. Cary's road and the River are ordered to clear it./.

Nov. 20, 1733 O.S., p. 219
Surveyor of the road
Henry Runnals is appointed Surveyor of the Road from the Mountains down the Country on the North side of the Northanna to meet Saunder's Road./.

20 Nov. 1733 O.S., p. 219
Hoggatt & c. to view road.
Anthony Hoggatt, & George Payne, Gent. are appointed to view the ground near the Plantation of Allen Howard, Gent. and report to the next Court which is the most convenient way for a road to pass through his land./.

20 Nov. 1733 O.S., p. 219
Womack to clear road.
On the motion of William Womack leave is granted him to clear a road from his Plantation into M^r. Cary's road./.

20 Nov. 1733. O.S., p. 219
Stoner to clear road.
On the motion of Daniel Stoner leave is granted him to clear a road from his Plantation into Mr. Cary's road./.

20 Nov. 1733 O.S., p. 219
Walker to clear road.
On the motion of Thomas Walker leave is granted him to clear a road from his Plantation into Mr. Cary's road./.

15 Jan. 1733 O.S., p. 221
Hoggatt & c. to view road.
Anthony Hoggatt, & George Payne Gent. make report which ground is most convenient for a road to pass near the Plantation of Allen Howard, M^r. Thomas Prosser as Attorney for the said Allen Howard opposes the road being carried according to their report but consents that it may be cleared between the said Howard's and William Knight's land to a Stone being one Corner of the land with which Thomas Saunder's Surveyor of the said road is satisfied on condition that the said Stone be not above 100 yards from the place where the lands of the said Howard & Knight joyn and it is ordered that the road be cleared according to that agreement./.

19 Feb. 1733 O.S., p.223
Road to be cleared.
Ordered that a road be cleared from Richard Parker's to the first Branch of Angola and Richard Ward is appointed Surveyor thereof./.

19 Feb. 1733 O.S., p. 223
Road to be altered.
Ordered that the road between little Licking hole & great Licking hole Creeks be turned nearer the foot of the hills./.

19 March 1733 O.S., p. 229
Road to be cleared.
On the motion of Thomas Dickins it is ordered that a bridle way be cleared from the lower Manakin Creek to the ffrench Church Edward Scott & William Sallee are appointed to lay of the said way and if they differ about it Peter Sublett is to determine the difference./.

19 March 1733 O.S., p. 233
Surveyor of the road.
Josiah Payne is appointed Surveyor of the road in the room of David Davis./.

21 May 1734 O.S., p. 253
Grand Jury's Presentments
...Surveyor of the Road from Tuckahoe to Bollings mill

21 May 1734 O.S., p. 253
Grand Jury's Presentments
...Surveyor of the Road from Bever dam Bridge to Bollings mill

21 May 1734 O.S., p. 253
Grand Jury's Presentments
...Surveyor of the Road from the Mountains to the head of Licking hole for not keeping the roads in repair.

21 May 1734 O.S., p. 253
Surveyor of Road.
Joseph Woodson is appointed Surveyor of the road from his Path to the County line on the South side of James River./.

21 May 1734 O.S., p. 254
Surveyor of the road.
Peter Jefferson is appointed Surveyor of the Road from the Mountains to Licking hole Creek in the room of Henry Runnalls./.

21 May 1734 O.S., p. 256
Road to be cleared.
Ordered that a road be cleared from the Court house to go upwards into the main Road & that John Webb Surveyor of the main road opposite to the Court House do clear the same./.

21 May 1734 O.S., p. 256
Road to be cleared.
Ordered that John Webb Surveyor of the main road do clear a road from the Court house upwards into the main road./.

16 July 1734 O.S., p. 273
Road to be cleared.
Ordered that a Road be cleared from the Round pond Road to Coll^o. John Carter's Plantation where Robert Davis is Overseer and Charles Lynch is appointed Surveyor of the said Road./.

16 July 1734 O.S., p. 275
Bridge to be built.
Ordered that Benjamin Moseby & John Saunders Surveyors of the Roads above & below Deep Creek do meet with their Gangs & make a Bridge over the said Creek./.

16 July 1734 O.S., p. 273
Surveyor of the Road.
Nicholas Cox is appointed Surveyor of the road in the roam of Jacob Winfrey and Marmaduke Hix./.

16 July 1734 O.S., p. 275
Bridge to be built.
Ordered that Benjamin Moseby & John Saunders Surveyors of the Roads above & below Deep Creek do meet with their Gangs & make a Bridge over the said Creek./.

17 Sept. 1734 O.S., p. 293
Surveyor of the Road.
Thomas Wadloe is appointed Surveyor of the Road in the room of Joseph Watkins./.

17 Sept. 1734 O.S., p. 293
Randolph to clear Road.
On the motion of William Randolph Junr. leave is granted him to a road from his dwelling house to Tuckahoe Mill./.

18 Sept. 1734 O.S., p. 294
Surveyor of the Road.
John Woodson is appointed Surveyor of the Road from Bever dam Bridge to Stony Creek./.

19 Nov. 1734 O.S., p. 309
Road to be cleared.
Ordered that a Road be cleared from the Court house Road where it comes into the River road to be continued to the ford at David Lyles's Daniell Stoner is appointed Surveyor thereof & the contiguous Surveyors & their Gangs are to assist in clearing the same./.

19 Nov. 1734 O.S., p. 310
Grand Jurys Presentm^{ts}.
I Peter Jefferson fforeman of the Grand Jury together with my fellow Jurors doe present as follows, We present the Overseers of the Road from the Court house to the fferry & from the fferry to the maine Road. Wee present the Overseers of the Road from the Court house to the Bird. We present the Overseer of the Road from Bever dam to Dover mill & the owner of Dover mill for not keeping the said mill dam in repair according to Law Ew^e. Scot & Tarlton Woodson Evidences. Wee present the Overseers of the Road from Little Creek to the Bird & from thence to Danl. Brits . . . Pet. Jefferson foreman.

19 Nov. 1734 O.S., p. 312
Bridge to be built.
Ordered that the Surveyor & his Gang below Deep Creek & the Surveyor & his Gang above the Creek do joyn in making a Bridge over the said Creek./.

19 Nov. 1734 O.S., p. 312
Bridge to be built.
Ordered that the Surveyor & his Gang below Muddy Creek & the Surveyor & his Gang above the Creek do joyn in making a Bridge over the said Creek./.

19 Nov. 1734 O.S., p. 312
Surveyor of the Road.
George Carrington is appointed Surveyor of the Road from Muddy Creek to Willis's Creek./.

19 Nov. 1734 O.S., p. 312
Surveyor of the Road.
Phillip Webber is appointed Surveyor of the Road from the widow Johnson's to the upper Tuckahoe Creek./.

19 Nov. 1734 O.S.; p. 312
Bridge to be built.
Ordered that workmen be treated with at the next Court for building a Bridge over the lower Tuckahoe Creek./.

19 Nov. 1734 O.S., p. 312
Surveyor of the Road.
Isham Randolph is appointed Surveyor of the Road from Little Licking hole to Webb's Spring./.

19 Nov. 1734 O.S., p. 312
Surveyor of the Road.
William Cabbell is appointed Surveyor of the Road from Webb's Spring to the Bird Creek./.

19 Nov. 1734 O.S., p. 312
Road to be cleared.
Ordered that William Womack & his Gang do clear a Road from the Glebe into the River Road towards the Church./.

21 Jan. 1734 O.S., p. 314
Road not to be esteemed publick.
Ordered that the Road from the round pond to the Secretary's Quarter be esteemed no Publick Road./.

21 Jan. 1734 O.S., p. 314
Surveyor of the Road.
Ordered that the same titheables appointed by the Vestry and the titheables on the South side of the North River above Barringer's be the Gang to work on the Road of which Peter Jefferson is Surveyor.

21 Jan. 1734 O.S., p. 314
Road to be cleared.
Ordered that a Road be cleared from Horseley's Bridge to the new Bridge at little licking hole Creek Arthur Hopkins is appointed Surveyor thereof & the titheables of Arthur Hopkins, John Mosebey, Martin Dunkin, George Southerland, Sylvester Prophet, Thomas Wharton, & John Richards are ordered to assist in clearing the same./.

21 Jan. 1734 O. S., p. 315
Road to be turned.
Ordered that leave be given the Surveyor of the Road from little licking hole to great licking hole to turn the road./.

21 Jan. 1734 O.S., p. 315
Road to be Cleared.
On the motion of Charles Hudson & others leave is granted them to clear a road from their Plantations in the ffork to the North River./

18 March 1734 O.S., p. 341
Surveyor of the Road.
Robert Carter is appointed Surveyor of the Road from Muddy Creek to Willis's Creek & the Road is Ordered to be cleared as it is laid out by George Carrington./.

18 March 1734 O.S., p. 342
Dover mill dam to be repaired.
William Randolph agrees to mend his Mill darn & to make it ten foot wide at top for which it is Ordered that two thousand pounds of tobacco convenient be leveyed him, and forever hereafter he agrees to keep the said dam in good repair according to law./.

19 March 1734 O.S., p. 344
Tuckahoe bridge to be built.
Anthony Hoggatt, George Payne, & Henry Wood are appointed to agree with workmen to build a Bridge over the lower Tuckahoe Creek and the agreement is to be made for money./.

19 March 1734 O.S., p. 345
Surveyor of Road.
Ordered that a Road be cleared from Henrico line over Butter wood to Jenitoe & Thomas Locket is appointed Surveyor thereof./.

19 March 1734 O.S., p. 345
Surveyor of Road.
John Worley is appointed Surveyor of the Road in the room of Joseph Woodson./.

20 March 1734 O.S., p. 350
Surveyor of Road.
William Randolph is appointed Surveyor of the Road from Buck Branch to Tuckahoe Bridge

20 May 1735 O.S., p. 354
Grand Jury vs. Bostick
On the Presentment of the Grand Jury against John Bostick Surveyor of the Road for not keeping his road in repair the Court having heard his excuse the presecution against him is dismist./.

20 May 1735 O.S., p. 355
Road to be viewed.
Ordered that Isham Randolph &. Tarlton ffleming Gent. do view the Road from the Court house fferry to the main road & report the same to the next Court./.

20 May 1735 O.S., p. 356
Surveyor of Road.
Joseph Baugh is appointed Surveyor of the Road in the room of John Worley./.

17 June 1735 O.S., p. 362
Surveyor of Road.
Dudley Digges Gent is appointed Surveyor of the road from mount Misery to the Bird all the Titheables between mount Misery and the Bird and the Titheables belonging to Miles Cary Gent. are ordered to work on the said road./.

17 June 1735 O.S., p. 362
Netherland to clear road
On the motion of John Netherland leave is granted him to clear a road from his House to the main road./.

16 Sept. 1735 O.S., p. 381
Surveyor of Road.
Henry Clay is appointed Surveyor of the Road in the room of Edmund Butler./.

16 Sept. 1735 O.S., p. 381
Surveyors of Road.
Thomas Edwards is appointed Surveyor of the Road from Dudley Digges's Plantation to Bear Creek, William Halliday is appointed Surveyor from Bear Creek to Watson's Quarter, Richard Parker Surveyor from Watson's Quarter to Coll^o. Eppes's path & Joseph Woodson Surveyor from Coll^o. Eppes's path to Let alone./.

16 Sept. 1735 O.S., p. 381
Surveyor of Road
Anthony Hoggatt is appointed Surveyor of the Road from Cary's path to Hoggatt's Mill & the tithables of Coll^o. Richard Randolph at his two upper Quarters, M^r. Henry Cary at his upper Quarter, & the tithables of M^r. Anthony Hoggatt are Ordered to clear the same./.

16 Sept. 1735 O.S., p. 382
Bridge to be built.
Ordered that a Bridge be built over Deep Creek and another over Muddy Creek at the charge of the County & that workmen do agree with the Court./.

16 Sept. 1735 O.S., p. 385
Road to be cleared.
Ordered that the John M^c.Brid & his Gang do clear the Road from the Court house towards Thomas Christian's./.

17 Sept. 1735 O.S., p. 391
Surveyor of Road.
Jacob Michaux is appointed Surveyor of the Road from the River to Napiers path./.

17 Sept. 1735 O.S., p. 391
Surveyor of Road.
ffrancis James is appointed Surveyor of the Road from the ffork of ffine Creek to Jacob Michaux's Road./.

Order Book 4, Goochland County

18 Nov. 1735 O.S., p. 2
Road to be viewed
Tarlton ffleming and Peter Jefferson Gent. are appointed to view the Road of Thomas Pleasants at Thomas Pleasants' Plantation and to direct it be turned if they think fitt.

18 Nov. 1735 O.S., p. 2
Surveyor off Road.
John Hide Saunders is appointed Surveyor of the road in the room of his ffather John Saunders./.

18 Nov. 1735 O.S., p. 3
Surveyor off Road.
Peter Ware is appointed Surveyor of the road from Dover Mill to Beverdam Bridge./.

19 November 1735 O.S., p. 23
ffleming &c to be sumd.
On the Motion of Jacob Michaux Surveyor of the Road it is ordered that John ffleming Samuel Vardry and John Netherland be Sumoned to appear at the next Court to shew cause why they don't send their Tithables to work on the road./.

25 Nov. 1735 O.S., (after a group of levies)
Isham Randolph Gent. moves that a bridge may be Built over Dover Mill Creek at the Charge of the County, which motion is rejected by the Court./.

25 Nov. 1735 O.S.,
Court for laying the annual County levy
Richard Moseby agrees to Build a Bridge over Deep Creek for Twenty pounds Currant Money and to keep it in repair Seven years and then leave it in repair./.

John Netherland agrees to build a Bridge over Muddy Creek for Twenty pounds Currant Money and to keep it in repair Seven years and then leave it in repair./.

Daniel Stoner George Carrington Gent. are to Direct Where the Bridges shall be Built./.

17 March 1735 O.S., p. 40
Surveyor of Road.
Samuel Allen Son of William Allen is appointed Surveyor of the Road. in the room of Nicholas Cox./.

18 March 1735 O.S., p. 47
fferry to be Kept
On the Motion of Edward Scott leave is granted him to Keep fferry on James River at the Manacan town opposite to Stephen Woodson's at the Same Rates with Woodson's fferry./.

18 March 1735 O.S., p. 47
fferry to be Kept
On the Motion of Jacob Michaux leave is granted him to Keep fferry on James River opposite to the Court house and the Same rate with the Court house fferry./

20 April 1736 O.S., p. 49
Road to be Cleared.
Ordered that a Bridge be Built over Deep Creek near where the Chappel Road Crosses, that William Mayo and Anthony Hoggatt. Gent do view the most Convenient Place and that Workmen be Treated with at the next Court./.

20 April 1736 O.S., p. 51
Road to be Cleared.
Ordered that the Tithables of Coll^o. Richard Randolph's two Quarters Capt. Moseley's Quarter, William Clay, Thomas Moor, and John Worley at Jenito Quarter, do work on the road whereof Henry Clay is Surveyor that John Baugh do clear the Road from Ditoways Branch to Watkin's Path and that Henry Clay Keep the bridge in repair./.

18 May 1736 O.S., p. 52
Surveyor of Road.
Nowell Burton is appointed Surveyor of the Road in the room of Samuel Allen Junr../.

18 May 1736 O.S., p. 53
Grand Jury Sworn...
...against Overseer of the road from the River road down to Sarah Johnson's Against the Road from Major Mayo's to the ridge Road Against the overseer of the road from Dover fferry to the main Road on North side the River. Against M^r. Scott for not Keeping Jones's Creek Bridge in Repair...

18 May 1736 O.S., p. 60
Netherland's bridge reced.
The Court are of opinion that the bridge built by John Netherland According to his Agreement is well and Sufficiently Performed and M^r. Shelton is hereby desired to Pay him out of the County money in his hands Twenty pounds Currant money./.

18 May 1736 O.S., p. 60
Moseby's bridge reced.
The Court are of opinion that the bridge built by Richard Moseby According to his Agreement is well and Sufficiently Performed and M^r. Shelton is hereby desired to pay him out of the County money in his hands Twenty Pounds Currant money

19 May 1736 O.S., p. 65
Bridges to be Built
Edward Scott Agrees to Build a Bridge over Deep Creek and one over little licking hole Creek for seven pounds Each and to keep the same in Repair Seven years, and the Court are of opinion that he undertake and finish the Same for which they hereby Engage to pay him the said Sums of Seven pounds Currant money for Each bridge./.

15 June 1736 O.S., p. 66
Bridges to be Built.
It is agreed that M^r. Edward Scott is not to make Causways to the Bridges he hath formerly undertaken to build for the County./.

17 June 1736 O.S., p. 77
Surveyor of Road.
Benjamin Bradshaw is appointed Surveyor of the Road in the Room of John Gunn./.

17 June 1736 O.S., p. 77
Surveyor of Road.
Edward Scott is appointed Surveyor to Clear a new Road from the North River up the ffork and Across Hardwarr River./.

20 July 1736 O.S., p. 88
Michaux's ordinary Lycense
On the motion of Jacob Michaux Lycense is granted him to keep an ordinary at his Ferry Arthur Hopkins entring himself Security for the same.

20 July 1736 O.S., p. 88
Michaux's Bond for fferry
Jacob Michaux enters into Bond according to Law for the well keeping of his fferry and Arthur Hopkins his Security.

21 Sept. 1736. O.S., p. 121
Surveyor of the road
Josias Payne is appointed Surveyor of the road in the room of John Laine and leave is granted him to turn the same.

21 Sept. 1736 O.S., p. 121
Surveyor of the road.
Charles Lynch is appointed Surveyor of the Mountain road in the room of Peter Jefferson.

21 Sept. 1736 O.S., p. 121
Surveyor of the road.
On their motion leave is granted the upper Inhabitants on the South River to clear a Road from Leonard Ballews upper Plantation to slate River.

17 May 1737 O.S., p. 139
Road to be Cleared.
Ordered that the Tithables of Henry Cary Gent be exempt from Clearing the New road over Willis's Creek.

17 May 1737 O.S., p. 139
Road to be Cleared.
Ordered that the Tithables below the Bridge over Deep Creek to the Chappel do assist John Twitty the Surveyor thereof.

17 May 1737 O.S., p. 139
Bird Creek Bridge.
Ordered that Tarlton ffleming and Peter Jefferson Gent. do view the large branch of the Bird Creek above the ffork and to report the value of a Bridge.

17 May 17.37 O.S., p. 139
Road to Be Cleared & Tithables
John Cobb is appointed Surveyor of the Road from Henry Webb's to the Bird Creek and it is ordered that his own Capt. Massies, James Sheltons Thomas Stones and Jonas Lawson's tithables do work on that Road. and it is ordered that Tithables without the Road are to be added to the Road of which Doctor Hopkins is Surveyor.

17 May 1737 O.S., p. 139
Road to be Clear'd
George Stovall is appointed Surveyor of the Road above Deep Creek Bridge on the Chappell Road to John Merrymans path.

17 May 1737, O.S., p. 139
Road to be Cleared & Tithables.
Ordered that the Tithables of William Battersby, Abraham Cowley, Thomas Wooldridge, and John Pankey do work on the road of which Joseph Baugh is Surveyor.

17 May 1737 O.S., p. 139
Road to be Cleared
Benjamin Wheeler is appointed Surveyor of part of the Mountain Road on the North side of James River beginning at Number Twelve and ending at Number Thirty.

17 May 1737 O.S., p. 139
Road to be Clear'd
On the motion of Michael Wood leave is granted him to Clear a road from the Blew Ledge of Mountains down to Ivy Creek.

18 May 1737 O.S., p. 145
Willis's Creek Bridge.
Anthony Hoggatt and George Carrington Gent are appointed to view a place over Willis's Creek for Building a Bridge and to agree with

an undertaker to build the bridge for a Sum not exceeding Twenty-five pounds that they shall do therein to the next Court.

19 May 1737 O.S., p. 148
Road to be Cleared
Thomas Turpin Gent Surveyor of the road from the Ordinary to the North fork of ffine Creek the upper bridge to be included and Maj^r. William Mayo's tithables are to be included in his gang.

19 May 1737 O.S., p. 148
Road to be Cleared
William Allen is appointed Surveyor of the ross[?] leading from the Court House to Appomattox River beginning at the Church road and thence to Mr. Cary's road. Col^o. Randolph's two Quarters where Scruggs and Lee are overseers are to be added to his gang.

19 May 1737 O.S., p. 148
Road to be Cleared
Phillip Thomas is Appointed Surveyor of that part of the road between M^r. Cary's road and Appomattox River and to cut the River banks.

19 May 1737 O.S., p. 148
Road to be Cleared.
John Hide Saunders is appointed Surveyor of the road from Deep Creek bridge to the Court house road.

19 May 1737 O.S., p. 160
Road to be Cleared.
William Womack is appointed Surveyor of the Road from the Manakin town fferry on the north side of James River to the main road.

20 May 1737 O.S., p. 161
Road to be Cleared
Ordered that the Road from the Court house fferry on the North Side the River to the main road be Cleared upon that ridge of land on which the house in which Joseph Woodson did dwell is built.

20 May 1737 O.S., p. 169
Road to be Cleared
Ordered that the road passing by the plantation of John Taylor be removed to pass over best the ground nearer the branch and that John Taylor do clear the same.

21 June 1737 O.S., p. 180
Road to be Cleard
John White is appointed Surveyor of the road from the falls of Hardwar to the north river to be Cleard the most Convenient way that can be, and it is ordered that the tithables on the branches of Hardwar do clear the same.

19 July 1737 O.S., p. 184
Surveyor of Road
Ordered that the old River Road from the Manacan town fferry downwards be opened, and M^r. William Randolph is appointed Surveyor thereof.

19 July 1737 O.S., p. 184
Surveyor of Road.
William Haris is appointed Surveyor of the Mountain road from Number forty to forty-six.

19 July 1737 O.S., p. 184
Bird Creeke Bridge.
Tarlton ffleming reports that he hath viewed the Bird Creek and that the place which he thinks proper for building a bridge over it is Sixty foot wide.

19 July 1737 O.S., p. 186
Willis's Creek Bridge
Ordered that George Carrington and Daniel Stoner Gent do view the most Convenient place on Willis's Creek over which a bridge may be built and to report the same to the next Court.

16 August 1737 O.S., p. 214
Surveyor of Road
William Randolph Gent is appointed Overseer of the road from Dover Mill to the Court House.

16 August 1737 O.S., p. 214
Parker's Ordin^y. Lycence.
On the motion of Thomas Parker fferrykeeper lycence is granted him to keep an Ordinary at Stephen Woodson deceas'd fferry According to Law, the ensuing Year, William Randolph entering himself Security for the same.

16 August 1737 O.S., p. 215
Willis's Creek Bridge.
Daniel Stoner and George Carrington Gent. are Appointed to agree with Workmen to Build a Bridge over Willis's Creek and to make report thereof to the next Court.

16 August 1737 O.S., p. 236
Bird Creek Bridge.
Ordered that Tarlton ffleming and Charles Lewis Gent. do agree with Workmen to Build a Bridge over the Bird Creek at the place that has been already viewed and to keep the same in repair Seven Years and to report their proceedings to the next Court.

20 Sept. 1737 O.S., p. 240
Survey^r of Road.
Ordered that William Allin do Clear the Road that he was appointed Surveyor of at May Court of trees, and then that he return with his Usual Gang to the Road that he was Surveyor of before.

20 Sept. 1737 O.S., p. 241
Surveyor of Road.
Thomas Turpin Gent. is appointed Surveyor of the Road from the Old Ordinary to the Bridge at long branch and is to have his former Gang.

20 Sept. 1737 O.S., p. 241
Lickinghole Creek Bridge.
Isham Randolph and Tarlton ffleming Gent are appointed to View and receive the Bridge Built over Lickinghole Creek if they approve the same to be Sufficient and it is ordered that the said Isham Randolph do pay unto Edward Scott ffifteen pounds Currant money for the same.

15 Nov. 1737 O.S., p. 252
Grand Jury's Presentments
…the Overseer of the Rod from Solomons Creek to fyne Creek, …

…the Overseer of Little Creek bridge Little Licking ho …

15 Nov.1737 O. S., p. 252
Willis's Creek Bridge.
Ordered that Capt. Isham Randolph do pay unto William Allin Twenty-five pounds Current Money for Building a Bridge over Willis's Creek.

21 Feb. 1737 O.S., p. 256
Manakin Town Road.
A Superseade e from the Governor to stay the Court's proceedings on the Manakin Town road is read.

21 March 1737 O.S., p. 258
Surveyor of Road.
Samuel Allen Junr. is appointed Surveyor of the Road in the room of Thomas Edwards.

21 March 1737 O.S., p. 258
Tuckahoe Bridge
Isham Randolph & Daniel Stoner Gent. are Appointed to meet the Gent. of Henrico Court to treat about the Building of a Bridge over Tuckahoe Creek and to report their proceedings to the next Court.

21 March 1737 O.S., p. 261
Taylor's Ordinary Lycense
On the motion of Charles Taylor fferryman Lycense is granted him to keep an Ordinary at the Manacan Town fferry according to Peter Martin entering himself Security for the same.

21 March 1737 O.S., p. 262
Willis's Creek Bridge.
Henry Cary Gent. proposeth to the Court that he will build a bridge over Willis's Creek and keep it in repair for one thousand pounds of Tobacco to be paid him Yearly, which proposition the Court take time to Consider.

16 May 1738 O.S., p. 291
Surveyor of Road.
John Wright is appointed Surveyor of the Road from a little below Number thirty six to his house.

16 May 1738. O. S., p. 292
Surveyor of Road.
John Robinson is Appointed Surveyor of the Road from his Path to Buckingham Road where Col°. Richard Randolph's road turns out and William Tabor is to direct the Carrying of the road.

16 May 1738 O.S., p. 294
Surveyors of Road.
Andrew Moreman is appointed Surveyor of the Mountain Road in the room of Charles Lynch, Benjamin Wheeler from Number twelve to Number twenty two and John Woody from Number twenty two to Number thirty.

16 Aug. 1738 O.S., p. 337
Surveyor of Road.
William Randolph Gent. is Appointed Surveyor of the Road from the fferry to Jones's Creek Bridge and from the Bridge to the County line.

19 Sept. 1738 O.S., p. 352
Surveyor of Road.
William Wamack Jun[r]. is Appointed Surveyor of the Road on the South side of James River leading towards the Head of Willis's River in the room of Anthony Hoggatt.

19 Sept. 1738 O.S., p. 358
Road to be Cleared.
On the Pet. of Robert Davis leave is granted him to Clear a Road from the Secretary's land on the mountains or the North River to his new Settlement on Tye River

19 Sept. 1738 O.S., p. 358
Road to be Cleared.
Ordered that a Road be Cleared from Willis's Creek Bridge to Bear Garden Creek and that George Carrington Gent. be Surveyor thereof, and from Bear Garden Creek to Sclate River and that David Pattison be Surveyor thereof, And from Sclate River Upwards, and that Allen Howard be Surveyor thereof.

20 Sept. 1738 O.S., p. 359
Beverdam Bridge.
John Woodson and Peter Jefferson Gent. are Appointed to View the Bridge over Beverdam Creek and to report the same to the next Court.

20 Feb. 1738 O.S., p. 371
Road to be Cleard.
Ordered that all the titheables above Sclate River except David Patteson and his Titheables do Clear the Road of which Allen Howard is Surveyor.

20 Feb. 1738 O.S., p. 371
Road to be Opened
Ordered that the road going thro'. Thomas Smith's Plantation at the Mountains be open be the Surveyor thereof.

20 Feb. 1738 O.S., p. 372
Road to be Cleared.
Ordered that the Titheables of John Anthony, ffras. Baker, Abraham Venable William Henderson, Robt. Kent, The^o. Hanks and Thomas Baily do Clear the Mountain Road from Number twenty two to number twenty six of which John Wooddy is Surveyor.

That the titheables of M^r. Smith, John Moss, Charles Massie, Willm. Atkinson Junr. John Walker on the Bird do Clear from number twenty six to number thirty of which Willm. Martin is Surveyor.

That all the Titheables on the North side the North River below Carrols Creek and below Bamboo Creek on the South side do Clear from number twelve to number twenty-two of which Benj^a. Wheeler is Surveyor.

That the Titheables of William Bailey, Robert Christian, Widow Christian Thomas Bibe, all the Owens, & Robert Lewis's do Clear the Road of which John Wright is Surveyor.

20 Feb. 1738 O.S., p. 373
Road to be Clear'd
On the motion of Joseph Bingley leave, is granted him to turn the road near where he now lives.

20 Feb. 1738 O.S., p. 373
Road to be Clear'd
Ordered that John Watson, Isaac Johnson, John Johnson, John Barnet- John ffarrar, Strangeman Hutchens, Joel Watkins & Thomas Joplin do assist Philip Webber Surveyor of the road in making a Bridge Over Tuckahoe Creek.

20 Feb. 1738 O.S., p. 373
Road to be Clear'd
On the motion of Henry Chiles leave is Granted him to Clear a Road from Brooks's mill to his Land on Appomattox River

20 Feb. 1738. O.S., p. 373
Surveyor of Road.
John Payne is appointed Surveyor of the road in the room of John Webb.

20 Feb. 1738 O.S., p. 374
Surveyor of Road.
John Barnit is appointed Surveyor of the Road in the room of Joseph ffarrar.

20 Feb. 1738 O.S., p. 374
Road to be Clear'd
John Bostick is appointed Surveyor of the Road from Great Guiney Creek to Carys Road. Ordered that all the Titheables on the north side the said Creek do Clear the same, and that the Joining Gang do Assist and joyn to make a Bridge over Great Guiney Creek.

20 Feb. 1738 O.S., p. 374
Road to be Clear'd
Ordered that a Road be Cleared from Jenetoe Creek to Appamatox River above M^r. Beverley Randolph's Plantation and that George Williamson be Surveyor thereof. the Tithables between Henrico County line and the River are Appointed to Clear the same.

20 Feb. 1738 O.S., p. 374
Surveyor of Road.
Charles Allen is Appointed Surveyor of the Road in the room of Willm. Harris

20 March 1738 O.S., p. 377
Road to be clear'd.
On the motion of Ralph fflippen leave is granted him to Clear a Bridle Road from his house on Muddy Creek into the Chappel road.

20 March 1738 O.S., p. 377
Road to be Cleard.
On the motion of Nowel Burton leave is granted him to Clear a road from his Plantation on Willis's Creek to a Plantation belonging to

M#r#. Dudley Digges Called Buckingham M#r#. Benjamin Harrison Approveing its going thro'. M#r# Henry Cary's Land.

20 March 1738 O.S., p. 378
Roads to be Posted
Pursuant to an Act of Assembly of this Colony it is Ordered that the Surveyors of the Severall Roads within this County where two or more Crossroads or highways meet do forthwith cause to be Erected in the most Convenient place where such ways joyn, A Stone or Post with Inscriptions thereon in large Letters directing to the most noted place to which each of the said Joyning roads leads

20 March 1738 O.S., p. 378
Road to be Clear'd.
David Walker is Appointed Surveyor of the Road from the meadow above John Curds to the Court house.

John Bibe is Appointed Surveyor of the road between the two roads to the Court house and Rob#t# Rogers's titheables be added to his gang.

Ordered that the road from the upper end of John Curds to the Lower end of Maj#r# Bolling's Plantation be stop't up and that James Nowling do continue his road to the floodgates of Maj#r#. Bolling's mill.

Joseph Bingley is Appointed Surveyor of the road from Jones's Creek Bridge to the County line in the room of M#r#. Randolph And that all the Titheables without the road do Assist him in clearing the same.

20 March 1738 O.S., p. 381
Surveyor of Road.
William Williams is Appointed Surveyor of the Road from Dover mill to Beverdam bridge

John Pollock is Appointed Surveyor of the Road Beverdam Bridge to the branch above the Courthouse in the room of William Randolph.

15 May 1739 O.S., p. 400
Scots Ordinary Lysense
On the motion of Ann Scott fferrykeeper leave is granted her to keep an Ordinary at the Manacanton fferry According to Law.

15 May 1739 O.S., p. 400
Surveyor of Road.
James Barnes is Appointed Surveyor of the Road from the Chappel to the Upper Bridge on the main Deep Creek.

15 May 1739 O.S., p. 403
Bridge to be Built.
Henry Wood, Peter Jefferson & Charles Lynch Gent. are Appointed to View the Creek and Report the most Convenient place Over My chunk to build a bridge and the value thereof to the next Court.

15 May 1739 O.S., p. 403
Road to be Viewed.
Tarlton ffleming Peter Jefferson Gent. are appointed to view the Road below Curds and to make their Report to the next Court.

17 July 1739 O.S., p. 420
Surveyor of Road.
Charles Spurlock is Appointed Surveyor of the road in the room of John Prior.

18 July 1739 O.S., p. 423
Surveyor of Road.
Ordered that the old Road near Maj^r. Bolling's mill be kept open, that James Nowling be Surveyor thereof, And that he repair the old Bridge, and the new road to be discontinued.

18 July 1739 O.S., p. 423
Road to be Clear'd.
Ordered that leave be given to Alexander Marshall to Clear a Road from his Mill into Skin Quarter road, and into Buckingham road.

18 July 1739 O.S., p. 423
Road to be Clear'd.
Ordered that Joseph Pace be Surveyor of the Road from the Bridge on the Bird Creek to the Crooked falls on the Rivanna the Titheables to work on the same are M^r. Grays, Coll^o. Martins, Bryan Conolly, Robt. Dute, Joseph Barringers, Benj^a. Hawkins, William May, John Denny, Chas. Lewis's at his mill Quarter.

Ordered that Thomas Harbour be Surveyor of the Road from M^r. Hopkins Quarter up the Ridge to My Chunk Creek and all the Titheables between the said Road and the River and on the South side the River do work on the said Road and Clear the same.

18 July 1739 O.S., p. 423
Bridge to be Built.
Thomas Pleasants agrees to Build a Bridge over Beverdam Creek and to keep the same in Repair fifteen Years from the finishing, for which the Court agrees to give him Twenty pounds Curr^t. money.

21 Aug. 1739 O.S., p. 433
Surveyor of Road.
Alexander Stinson is Appointed Surveyor of the Road from Brooks's mill to Arthers, his gang to be Willm. Grays Tiths, Peter Brooks, John Hodnet, John Harmer, John Payne, James Glen, Henry Carys tiths, William Cook, and Richard Henderson. And William Wamack jun^r. gangs to be Chas. Anderson, Thos. Hodges, Henry, Joseph & James Cary, William Kent, Robert Peak, William Easley, Alex^r. Trents Q^r. John Arthers Q^r. Edward M'gehe, James Allens Q^r. William Mills and John Ownby.

21 Aug. 1739 O.S., p. 433
Road to be Cleard.
Ordered that Silvanus Maxey have leave to Clear a Bridle way from where Maj^r. Mayos road turns into the Chappel road to go by James Gate's and from thence to directed by James Watkins and Edwd. Tanner to Edwd. Maxeys.

18 Sept. 1739 O.S., p. 438
Surveyor of Road.
George Williamson is Appointed Surveyor of the Road from the County line in Lockets road to Appamatox River above Beverly Randolphs Quarter, And the Titheables between the line, the road and the River are to Clear the same.

17 Dec. 1739 O.S., p. 445
County Levy Court, 1739 (Lists of tobacco paid out)
To Anthony Hughes for one Post with 4 arms 40
To John Williams for three Posts with 6 Boards...80
To William Holladay for one Post...20
To Joseph Bingley for one Post...25
To John Pollock for five Posts and 10 boards...10
To Benj^a. Bradshaw for one D^o. and 2 boards...20
To David Walker for three D^o. and 6 boards...60
To Willm. Williams for one D^o. and 2 boards...30
To John Radford for one D^o. and 2 boards...30
To Joseph Pace for two and 4 boards...60
...John Harris for one and 2 boards...30
...To ffra^s. James for six...16 boards...480

18 Dec. 1739 O.S., p. 448
Road to be Cleared...
Ordered that a Road be Cleared from a little above Allen Howard's towards Brook's Spring in Hanover County And that Charles Allen and his Gang do clear the same.

18 Dec. 1739 O.S., p. 450
Surveyor of Road.
ffrederick Cox is Appointed Surveyor of the road from Solomons Creek to fine Creek.

18 Dec. 1739 O.S., p. 450
Jones's Creek Bridge.
Tarlton ffleming and Thomas Turpin Gent. are Appointed to agree with Workmen to Build a Bridge over Jones's Creek.

19 Feb. 1739 O.S., p. 452
Jones's Creek Bridge.
The Court agree to give ffra^s. James Twelve pounds Curr^t. money for building a Bridge over Jones's Creek and to keep the same in repair Seven Years.

15 April 1740 O.S., p. 455
Cox's Ord. Lycense*
On the motion of John Cox fferrykeeper Lycense is granted him to keep an Ordinary at the Manacan Town fferry According to Law. Joseph Scott enters himself Security for the same.

15 April 1740 O.S., p.456
Road to be Cleared.
On the Petition of Norvel Burton, Thos. Christian, Jos: Hunter Benjamin Witt, Auth^o. Bening, John James Solager, Meridith Maning, Peter Chastain, James Wodkins, Auth^o. Vilen & Joseph Bening leave is granted to Clear a road out of the Chapple road, to extend along Capt. Bernerds road and from thence a Cross Willis's River near the road Clear'd by Norvel Burton to Buckingham & Crossing the Head of Randolphs Creek into Glovers road near to Hatchers Creek Mountains. Ordered that the Petitioners, Thomas Turpins, Robert Bernerds Richard Burtons, Thiths do clear the same And that William Allen be Surveyor thereof.

15 April 1740 O.S., p. 456
Surveyor of Road.
John Payne is appointed Surveyor of the road near the Court house to the fferry, Ord^d. that his Own, William Grays, John Cannons, Edward Carter Joseph Woodsons Deced & John Richardsons Tiths do clear the same and make Causways for foot People.

19 May 1740 O.S., p. 460
Appamatox River Bridge
John ffleming, Daniel Stoner, and Tarlton ffleming Gent. are appointed to view the place and meat the Gent. of Amelia County to Consider about the Building a bridge over Appamatox River.

19 May 1740 O.S., p. 462
Surveyor of Road.
William Sallee is appointed Surveyor of the Road on the South side of James River in the room of William Randolph Gent.

19 May 1740 O.S., p. 462
Grand Jurys's Presentments
The Overseer of the Road from Little Creek to Beverdam for not keeping the Diricting Post.

The Oversearer of the Road from John Rights down to Curds Bridge.
The Oversearer of the Road from the fferry to Jno. Cocks.

21 May 1740 O.S., p. 468
Jones' Creek Bridge.
Ffra^s. James Reports to the Court that he finished the Bridge which he was to build by Agreement over Jones Creek the fourteenth day of April last from wh^{ch}. time he is to keep the same in Repair Seven Years.

22 May 1740 O.S, p. 489
Megginson to Clear road.
On the motion of William Megginson leave is granted him to Clear a road from his house to Willis's River Bridge.

17 June 1740 O.S., p. 489
Beverdam Bridge.
The Court Impower Col^o. William Randolph Junr. to take up money on Interest to pay M^r. Thom^s. Pleasants twenty pounds for building a Bridge over Beverdam Creek and keeping it in Repair for fifteen Years from this day.

17 June 1740 O.S., p. 490
Mychunk Bridge.
Workmen are Appointed to appear at the next Court to undertake the Building a Bridge over Mychunk Creek.

15 July 1740 O.S., p. 494
Road to be Clear'd. .
On the Petition of James Martin, John MCCord, Thos. Morrison, James Robinson, John Reid, Samuel & James Bell, John Weads, John & James Daben William Verdeman, John Small and Lazarus Small leave is granted them to Clear a Road from the Thorrowfare a little above Morrisons to the Secretarys fford.

15 July 1740 O.S., p. 495
Surveyor of Road.
Joseph Anthony is Appointed Surveyor of the Road in the room of John White.

15 July 1740 O.S., p. 495
Bridge to be built
The Court agree with ffrans James to Build a bridge over Mychunk Creek for Twenty pounds Curr^t. money. and to be discharg'd from keeping the same in Repair on the Delivery thereof.

15 July 1740 O.S., p. 499
Surveyor of Road.
Obediah Woodson is Appointed Surveyor of the Road from Brooks mill to the fork of Appamatox River

19 Aug. 1740 O.S., p. 510
Road to be Clear'd.
Ord^d. that a Road be Cleared from Maj^r. Stoner's Road to Lyles's fford on Appamatox River.

18 Nov. 1740 O.S., p. 518
Surveyor of road.
Richard Moseby is Appointed Surveyor of the road in the room of Benjamin Moseby.

17 March 1740 O.S., p. 596
Road to be Cleared.
Joel Chandler is Appointed Surveyor of that part of the road from Lyles's fford lying between the Chapple road and Deep Creek roads

By the desire of the Honble William Randolph Esqr. he is Appointed Surveyor of the road from the Chappel road to Lyles's fford.

Ord^d. that the Titheables within the Chapple road do Clear and Grubb same.

Nicholas Davies is Appointed Surveyor of the road from Muddy Creek on the River road to Willis's River Bridge and leave is granted him to turn the road.

Ordered that the road be Cleared from the Secretarys mill to the Lower main road to the Manacan Town fferry and that Chas. Jordan be Surveyor thereof.

ordered that Wamacks gang do Assist in opening the said road.

Ordered that Anthony Pouncy do open the road the old way through his Plantation which led into Hanover.

Tarlton Woodson Junr. is appointed Surveyor of the road from Dover mill to Beverdam Bridge.

17 March 1740 O.S., p. 596
Lickinghole bridge
The Court agree with Coll^o. Isham Randolph to build a bridge over little Lickinghole for ffour pounds Curr^t money.

16 June 1741 O.S., p. 540
Surveyor of road.
John Witt is appointed Surveyor of the road from Jones Creek bridge to ffine Creek.

21 July 1741 O.S., p. 565
Surveyor of road.
Ordered that Robert Sanders be Surveyor of the road from Barnets road to horn Quarter fford on Willis River. And Anthony Benin be Surveyor from Willis River upwards.

Order Book 5, Goochland County

15 Sept. 1741 O.S., p. 3
Road to be Clear'd
On the Petition of James Bell, William Verdeman, William Miller, Peter Hairston, Edward Molloy, Thomas Bell, James Bell, Junr. John & Thomas & Hugh Dobbins, Thomas & Charles Hughes, William White, Davis Stockdon, Alexander Reid, John Heard, Samuel Bell, William Morrison, John Roberts, David Martin, James Armour, James Robertson, John ffulton, Geo: Powel, John McCord, Saml. Arnett, Richard Stockdon, Thomas Stockdon & Hum Dobbins. Leave is given them to Clear a road from Thomas Morrisons to the D.S. tree in Michael Woods road. And that the Petitioners be exempt from working on any other road.

On the Petition of David Lewis, George Taylor, William Hargis, Samuel Stiles, James ffidler, Hugh ffrazier, Howard Cash, James Treland, David Lewis, Junr., Chas. Caffry David Rees, William Lewis, Abraham Slaten, & William Williams. leave is granted them to Clear a road from the Secretarys fford to the D.S. tree. And that the Petitioners be exempt from working on any other road.

On the Petition of Michael Woods, John Woods, William Woods, Archibald Woods, Michael Woods Junr. William Wallace, Dennis Doyle, John Jemison Saml. Jemison, Henry Baily, Andrew Wallace, Andrew McWilliams, Robert McNeely, James Henderson & James Kinkead leave is given them to Clear a road from the D.S. tree to Michael Woods And that the Petitioners be exempt from working on any other road.

15 Sept. 1741 O.S., p. 5
Surveyor of Road.
Anthony Bennin is appointed Surveyor of the Road from Barnets road over Willis River at Horn Quarter fford to Glovers road. And that Benj^a. Harrisons, James Watkins, Benjaman Witt, Peter Chastain, Meridith Manning, Capt. Barnets Nowel Burton, Richard Burton, Alexander Trent's, Uriah Print, Jacob Winfrey, Samuel Allin, Robert Sanders and their Titheables do Clear the same.

15 Sept. 1741 O.S., p. 5
Road to be opened.
Ordered that the old road over Deep Creek in the Chapple be opened and that James Barnes and George Stovals Gangs do open the same.

15 Sept. 1741 O.S., p. 6
Road to be Grubb'd
Ordered that the Gangs under ffred. Cox and Anthony Hughes do joyn & grubb the road from the Chapple road to Deep Creek Road.

15 Sept. 1741 O.S., p. 6
Road to be Clear'd.
Ordered that leave be given the Honble John Carter Esqr. to Clear a road from his Tye River Quarters to his Clear mount Quarters.

Ordered that a road be Cleared from the head of Letalone into the Chapple road near the Chapple

John Lain is appointed Surveyor of the road from John Curds to Ja^s. Christians.

Ordered that leave be given John Henry to Clear a Bridge road from Mountain road to Barrengers on the Rivanna.

17 Nov. 1741 O.S., p. 10
Road to be turned.
On the motion of Ralph Graves leave is granted him to turn the road going thro'. his land to the Glebe the most Conveinents way.

17 Nov. 1741 O.S., p. 10
Surveyor of Road.
John Williams is Appointed Surveyor of the road in the room of William Wamack.

17 Nov. 1741 O.S., p. 11
Bridge to be Built.
The Court agree with Benjamin Moseby for fifty shillings to set up the old Bridge over Deep Creek in Case Scotts Executrix is not oblig'd to rebuild the same.

17 Nov. 1741 O.S., p. 13
Road to be Clear'd.
Ordered that the Titheables between Great Guinea Creek and Green Creek do Clear the road from Great Guinea Creek to the mouth of the first branch of Angola Creek. And that Richard Ward be Surveyor thereof.

15 Dec. 1741 O.S., p. 19
Surveyor of Road.
James Bryan is Appointed Surveyor of the road in the room of Joseph Bingley.

16 March 1741 O.S., p. 21
Surveyor of Road.
Peter Martin is appointed Surveyor of the road from Jones Creek to fine Creek.

16 March 1741 O.S, p. 23
Surveyor of Road.
John Richardson is Appointed Surveyor of the road in the room of John Bide.

16 March 1741 O.S., p. 25
Road to be Viewed.
Ordered that ffran^s. James Stephen Bedford Thos. Turpin and Samuel Scott Gent. do view the ground the most Conveinents way for making a new road from Paul Michaux into the main road going down the Country to fall into the main road below Stephen Hughes and make report to the next Court.

16 March 1741 O.S., p. 26
Road to be Cleared.
Ordered that a Road be Cleared the most Conveinent and best way from Lickinghole Chapple into the Mountain road between Number thirty and thirty two.

Ordered that William Cabbell Gent. have leave to Clear a road from his house to Lickinghole Chapple.

19 April 1742 O.S., p. 27
(listing of petitions)
A Petition for fferry over the River at James Hendlys is read and ordered to be Certified

A Petition for fferry at Elk Island is read and ordered to be Certified.

...fferry at Tucker Woodsons is read and ordered to be Certified.

...fferry at Bennet Goods is read and ordered to be Certified.

A Petition for fferry from Richard Moseby's to Tarlton fflemings is read and ordered to be Certified to the General Assembly.

20 April 1742 O.S., p. 28
Surveyor of Road.
Young Stokes is Appointed Surveyor of the road in the room of Joseph Woodson.

18 May 1742 O.S., p. 45
Surveyor of Road.
Thomas Ballew is Appointed Surveyor of the road from Sclate River Opposite to his house. And William Pirkins from thence upwards.

15 June 1742 O.S., p. 58
Appamatox River Bridge.
John ffleming and Wade Netherland Gent. are Appointed to meet Edward Booker Gent. one of the Justices of Amelia Court to View the place for Building a Bridge over Appamatox River, and make report thereof to the next Court.

15 June 1742 O.S., p. 59
Road to be Viewed.
James Holman and Joseph ffarrar are Appointed to View the old road, and the new road Clear'd by m^r. Graves and report the same to the next Court.

16 June 1742 O.S., p. 75
Ward to Clear Road.
On the motion of Richard Ward leave is granted him to Clear a road from the Plantation where he now lives to his Plantation on Green Creek

20 July 1742 O.S., p. 84
Appamatox_Bridge.
Benjamin Cocke Gent. is appointed to meet Edward Booker Gent. to view the place for Building a bridge over Appamatox River and to make report thereof to the next Court.

20 July 1742 O.S., p. 85
Willis River Bridge.
Ordered that George Carrington, Stephen Bedford, James Nevil and Robert Hughes or any two of them do view the bridge over Willis River and make report thereof to the next Court.

21 July 1742 O.S., p. 98
Surveyor of road.
James Martin is appointed Surveyor of the road from Morrison's to Davis Stockdons, and Samuel Arnold from thence to the D. S. tree.

21 July 1742 O.S., p. 101
Road to be Cleard
On the motion of Tucker Woodson leave is granted him to Clear a road from his fferry into the Mountain road.

21 Sept. 1742 O.S., p. 111
Surveyor of Road.
Ordered that Howard Cash be Surveyor of the road from Buffelo Quarter to Tye River, Thomas Jones from Tye River to Rock fish. John Jones from Rock fish to Hardwar River. And that Peter Jefferson and Charles Lynch Gent. do settle their several Gangs.

Ordered that Thomas Martin be Surveyor of the road from Martin Kings to the Mountain ridge road all the Titheables between the two roads as high as Robert Adam's and as low as William Witts are appointed his gang to Clear the same.

Peter Jefferson Gent. is appointed Surveyor of the road in the room of Benjamin Wheeler.

Charles Lynch Gent. is appointed Surveyor of the road in the room of Edwin Hickman.

21 Sept. 1742 O.S., p. 112
Bird. Bridge.
The Court agreed to give Joseph Pace Twenty pounds Curr^t. money in consideration of his building again the Byrd Bridge and keeping it in repair so long a time as is between the last of August was Twelve months and the expiration of the seven years for which his bond is taken.

21 Sept. 1742 O.S., p. 113
Surveyor of road.
Sanburn Woodson is appointed Surveyor of the road from Paul Michaux to John Hide Sanders's the Inhabitants from Doct^r. Gays's Quarter to Anthony Morgans Inclusively to Clear the same.

ffrancis James is appointed Surveyor of the road from Paul Michaux to where the roads meet just above fine Creek on Stephen Hughes's road all the hands from Pleasants Quarter above fine Creek to Paul Michaux within the road (except Jacob Michaux's) to clear the same and that Sanburn Woodsons gang do help to Clear the new part of the road from Paul Michaux to the fork of the road.

19 Oct. 1742 O.S., p. 132
Surveyor of Road.
Samuel Ridgway is appointed Surveyor of the road in the room of Isham Randolph Gent.

William Radford is appointed Surveyor of the middle road in the room of James Nowling.

Ordered that a road be Clear'd & extended along the Chapple road to Robert Sanders's old Plantation on Bernards road and from 'thence along the ridge between Deep Creek and Muddy Creek into Buckingame road and that James Daniel be Surveyor thereof & that the old road going by Bradshaws be discontinued.

19 Oct. 1742 O.S., p. 133
Surveyor of road.
John Watson is app^d. Surveyor of the road in the room of W. Holladay

19 Oct. 1742 O.S., p. 137
Road to be Cleard.
Ordered that a road be Clear'd from Bennet Goods fferry Landing on the North side James River into the main road, also from his Landing on the South side into the main road. Col^o. William Randolph and Capt. Benjamin Cocke are Appointed to View the ground on the North side between the main road and Raines road and make report to the next Court.

19 Oct. 1742 O.S., p. 138
Road to be Cleard.
Ordered that a road be Cleard from near the Chapple into ffighting Creek road at or near the Negros Arm and that the Petitioners clear the same.

18 Oct. 1742 O.S., p. 156
County levy court 1742
Tucker Woodson is Appointed to keep the County fferry from XVIIIth. day of November MDCCXLII at Two Thousand pounds of Tobacco & Cask/Annum and Paul Michaux is to receive his part of the Tobacco in proportion to the time his Boat shall be in Use. The Sheriffs, Coroners, Constables, Prisoners and Guards to be sent over fferry free.

16 Nov. 1742 O.S., p. 159
Surveyor of road.
Charles Turnbull is appointed Surveyor of the road in the room of Charles Jordan. ordered that Ralph Graves's gang do assist the old gang to Clear the same.

On the motion of Roert Hughes Leave is granted him to Clear a road from his Quarter at Muddy Creek into the main road.

The road going from the Gleeb to the Church is to be kept in repair by Ralph Graves Surveyor.

John Richardson is Appointed Surveyor of the road from Bollings to Licking hole in the room of John Bibe.

16 Nov. 1742 O.S., p. 159
Grand Jury Sworn
...We present the Justices of Goochland Court for not making an order for Clearing Rivers & Creeks. We present the Surveyor of the road from Deep Creek Chapple to the ffork of Sclate River. We Present the Surveyor of the road from Dover mill to Beverdam M[r]. Arthur Hopkins Evidence. We present the Surveyor of the road from Bollings mill to Lickinghole. M[r]. Arthur Hopkins Evidence. We present the Surveyor of the road from Deep Creek Bridge to Barnets road. ...

16 Nov. 1742 O.S., p. 160
Road to be viewed.
Ordered that William Randolph and James Holman Gent do view the ground between the Manacanton fferry and Hoggatts Mill and report to the next Court the most conveinents way for a road.

16 Nov. 1742 O.S., p. 162
Road to be Clear'd.
Ordered that a road be Clear'd from Tye River to Waltons ffork of Sclate River and from thence into Glovers road.

On the motion of Wade Netherland Gent. leave is granted him to Clear a road from his house to the fferry.

21 Dec. 1742 O.S., p. 181
Road to be Clear'd.
Ordered that the Road be Opened from Mosbys fferry on the North side the River to Coll^o. Isham Randolphs road and that the new road and the old one into the main road be kept in repair by the Titheables of M^{rs}. Randolph, Tarlton ffleming Joseph Jackson and Thomas Carter, and that Tarlton ffleming be Surveyor thereof.

Ordered that Capt. Mosby with the Titheables belonging to his road do open the road from his fferry on the South side the River to the main road.

21 Dec. 1742 O.S., p. 181
Surveyor of Road &^{c}.
Robert Willis Junr. is Appointed Surveyor of the Road in the room of Richard Wade. Ordered that Maj^r. ffleming & Capt Bedford do View the road between Robert Hughes & John Nichols and make report to the next Court.

Ordered that the Path down the River from Buck Island to John Witts be kept open round the Plantations on the River by the Titheables of each Plantation.

21 Dec. 1742 O.S., p. 182
Mosby to clear a path.
On the motion of Jacob Mosby leave is granted him to clear a bridle path from his house between Deep Creek and horsepen branch into the main road. And that William Moss be Sumoned to appear at the next Court to make his objections thereto.

18 Jan. 1742 O.S., p. 192
Road to be Clear'd
John Smith is appointed Surveyor of the road from his house to William Wards to clear the same with his own Tithables and he is exempted from working on any other road.

Ordered that M^r. Graves, M^r. Barrets and John Roberts's Titheables do clear the road whereof John Richardson is Surveyor.

On the motion of Joseph Dabbs leave is granted him to Clear a road from his house into Coll^o. Rich^d. Randolphs road.

On the motion of Anthony Hoggatt leave is granted him to Clear a road from his house on Appamatox River into the road to be Cleared by Joseph Dabbs.

18 Jan. 1742 O.S., p. 192
Road to be viewed.
Ordered that Richard Parker Charles Anderson and James Terry do view the road from Buckingame road to Green Creek and make report thereof to the next Court.

15 March 1742 O.S., p. 195
Surveyor road.
William Walton is Appointed Surveyor of the River road from the Byrd to John Smiths Plantation.

17 May 1743 O.S., p. 220
Surveyor of road.
James Johnson is appointed Surveyor of the road in the room of Benjamin Bradshaw.

17 May 1743 O.S., p. 222
Surveyor of Road.
Ordered that the road be Kept Continued from Angola Creek to the ffork of Green Creek and that James Brown be Surveyor thereof.

Ordered that James Daniel be Surveyor of the road from his house to Willis's River on Buckingham road.

18 May 1743 O.S., p. 237
Road to be Cleared.
Ordered that John Hyde Sanders do clear a road from near his house to Cross the Chapple road and fall into Liles's road or Coll°. Randolphs Charriot road. Anthony Hughes's gang are to help open that part from the Chapple road to Liles's &^{c}.

19 May 1743 O.S., p. 241
Road to be Clear'd.
Leave is granted to Nowel Burton to Clear a road from his house over Willis's River at the Bridge built by the said Burton & Samuel Allin into Bernards road.

21 June 1743 O.S., p. 248
Road to be Clear'd.
On the motion of James ffendly leave is granted him to Clear a road from his fferry to Thomas Jones's.

21 June 1743 O.S., p. 249
Road to be Clear'd.
On the motion of Richard Mosby Gent. leave, is granted him to Clear a road from Jacob Michaux's Plantation to fall into the Church road between William Roberts's and Hezekiah Mosby.

21 June 1743 O.S., p. 253
Road to be Cleard.
On the motion of Ralph Graves it is ordered that William Sampson & Richard Crouch do Assist in Clearing the road of which he is Surveyor.

22 June 1743 O.S., p. 266
Surveyor of Road.
Nathl. Graves is Appointed Surveyor of the Road in the room of Chas. Lynch Gent

20 Sept. 1743 O.S., p. 272
Appamatox Bridge.
The Court are of Opinion over Appamatox River from the Land of William Bass to the Land of George Williamson Proposed to be Built by the Court of Amelia County is no way Necessary to the Inhabitants of Goochland and therefore do refuse to joyn with the Court of Amelia in building a Bridge at that place.

William Mayo and George Carrington Gent. say they do not refuse to build a Bridge at the said place.

20 Sept. 1743 O.S., p. 274
Alexander to open way.
On the motion of John Alexander leave is granted him to open a bridle way from his Plantation into the River road near M^{rs}. Randolph's Quarter. Stephen Bedford and Samuel Scott Gent. are Appointed to View the same.

20 Sept. 1743 O.S., p. 274
Surveyors of Roads.
George Williamson is Appointed Surveyor of Jenetoe road to Appamatox River.

Stephen Cox is Appointed Surveyor of the Road in the room of Young Stokes.

Robert Thompson is Appointed Surveyor of the Road in the room of the Honble William Randolph Esqr. deced.

Stephen Bedford Gent. is Appointed Surveyor of the road Deep Creek Bridge to Bates's House.

David Towns is Appointed Surveyor of the Road from Bates's house to ffine Creek.

John Harris is Appointed Surveyor of the Road from ffine Creek to Jones's Creek.

William Woodson is Appointed Surveyor of the Road from Dovermill to Beverdam.

David Lewis is Appointed Surveyor of the Road from the D.S. Tree down to Moors Creek and into the Secretarys Road and that the Tithables near the said road do clear the same.

Leave is granted Nicholas Davies Gent. to Open and Continue a River Road from Glovers old Plantation upwards as far as he thinks fit.

21 Sept. 1743 O.S., p. 292
Surveyor of Road.
Benjamin Harris is Appointed Surveyor of the Road from Jones's Creek Bridge to the Lower Manakin Creek.

18 Oct. 1-743 O.S., p. 294
Surveyor of Road.
Henry Martin is Appointed Surveyor of the Road from M^r. Hopkins Quarter to Barringers Creek.

Thomas Harbour is Appointed Surveyor of the Road from Barringers Creek to the Mountain Road.

Ordered that John ffranklins and John Bates's Tithables do work on the. Road under Stephen Bedford Gent. Surveyor.

15 Nov. 1743 O.S., p. 306
County Levy Court. 1743
To [Tucker Woodson] for keeping fferry twelve month ffrom Novem. 18 1742
                                                            1,000 [pounds of tobacco]
                                                            Cask 40 [pounds of tobacco]
To Paul Michaux for D^o. twelve months   1,000 [pounds of tobacco]
                                                            Cask 40 [pounds of tobacco]

15 Nov. 1743 O.S., p. 307
County Levy Court. 1743
To Robert Hughes for Timber for Bridge   24 [pounds of tobacco]
To ffrancis James for putting up 4 Arms & 2 Posts   100 [pounds of tobacco]

15 Nov. 1743 O.S., p. 308
County Levy Court. 1743
To Daniel Johnson for Timber for Bridge over Solomons Creek   32 [pounds of tobacco]

Ordered that Two Thousand pounds of Tobacco and Casks be Allowed to Tucker Woodson, Paul Michaux, Jacob Michaux and William Burks the four fferry keepers equal it to be Divided or to those shall do the Service of the County and Parrish fferry keeper.

15 Nov. 1743 O.S., p. 310
Surveyor of Road.
Israel Winfry is Appointed Surveyor of the Road in the room of Joseph Baugh.

15 Nov. 1743 O.S., p. 310
Mosbys fferry Landing to be Viewed.
Arthur Hopkins, Benjamin Cocke & William Cabell Gent. are Appointed to View the Landings on both sides the River at Mosbys fferry and Report to the next Court which is the most Conveinents place.

15 Nov. 1743 O.S., p. 322
Surveyor of Road
William Burk is Appointed Surveyor of the Road in the room of John Payne.

15 Nov. 1743 O.S., p. 321
Road to be Viewed.
On the Petition of Alexander Trent praying that the road which now goes through his Lowgrounds on Willis's Creek South branch may be altered. It is Ordered that Charles Anderson, Obediah Woodson and Stephen Sanders do view the old road and the land through which the new road is intended to be Cleared and make report which they find most Convenient to next January Court.

20 Dec. 1743 O.S., p. 328
Road to be Clear'd.
Ordered that a Road be Cleard from Lickinghole Chapple into the Mountain Road and that Thomas Sanders be Surveyor thereof.

20 Dec. 1743 O.S., p. 329
Road to be Cleared.
On the motion of Jacob Michaux leave is granted him to turn the road to the fferry Landing through his own land.

    Ordered that the Secretarys road be continued from Tye River to ffendlys Gap on the Little Mountains and from thence the nearest way to the South River.

    John Owen is appointed Surveyor of the road to Lyles's fford in the room of Robert Thompson.

20 March 1743 O.S., p. 343
Deep Creek Bridge.
John ffleming Nicholas Davies & Isaac Bates Gent. or any two of them are Appointed to treat and agree with workmen for the Rebuilding of Deep Creek Bridge and to make report to the Court.

20 March 1743 O.S., p. 344
Road to be Cleard.
William Randolph Junr. is Appointed Surveyor of Buckingham road from John Mossoms to Letalone Quarter and that his own John Povals and the rest of the Tiths below ffighting Creek Conveinent to the said Road are to Clear the same.

    John Owen is Appointed Surveyor of the road from Lyles's fford to the Chapple road and that those Tiths in the precincts of the said road who do not work under M^r. William Randolph do Clear the same.

    Ordered that the Tithables Convenient to the road of which Capt. James Martin is Surveyor do work on the said road.

    Ordered that the Tithables Conveinent to the road of which Samuel Arnold is Surveyor do work on the said road.

20 March 1743 O.S., p. 346
Surveyor of Road.
Thomas Ballew is Appointed Surveyor of the road from Glovers old Plantation above Willis's to Georges Branch.

    William Perkins is Appointed Surveyor of the Road from Georges Branch to or near Scicamore Island Creek.

    Samuel Spencer is Appointed Surveyor of the Road from Scicamore Island Creek and to fall on Negro Creek between Sclate River Mountain and the ffluvanna.

    James Spencer is Appointed Surveyor of the road from Glovers Plantation so farr 'till he meets Thomas Ballew.

    Abraham Childers is Appointed Surveyor of the road from Willis's Bridge to Thompson's branch.

    John Cannon is Appointed Surveyor of the load from Thompson's branch to Bear Garden Creek.

    Ordered that the Tithables that are Conveinent to and did formerly work on the road Called Bradshaws road do work on and Clear the new road of which James Daniel is Surveyor.

23 March 1743 O.S., p. 370
Surveyor of Road.
John Holland is Appointed Surveyor of the road in the three notch'd road to the Chapple.

15 May 1744 O.S., p. 386
Grand jury Sworn
…We Present Charles Allin for not Clearing the road he is Surveyor of the three notch'd road from N°. 40 to 46. We Present the Surveyor of the road from John Mossoms to the Head of Dutoys branch for not Clearing the-said Road by the Information of Silvanus Maxey. We Present the Surveyor of the road from Jacob Michaux's to Bates's house for not Clearing the said Road. We Present the Surveyor of the Road from John Mossom to Lettalone for not Clearing the same. …

15 May 1744 O.S., p. 388
Surveyor of road.
James ffendly is Appointed Surveyor of the road from his fferry to Thomas Jones's.

Ordered that Samuel Stephens John ffendly Thos. Watts Major Lewis Hugh Dennum John Isham Archibald Blake David Griffin James ffreeland Henry Johnson & Charles Burk do work on the said road.

16 May 1744 O.S., p. 395
Surveyor of Road.
Edwin Hickman Gent. is Appointed Surveyor of the Road from My Chunk Creek to the Secretarys fford.

James Hopper is Appointed Surveyor of the Road from the Upper ffork of Licking hole to the Little Byrd in the room of Josias Payne.

17 May 1744 O.S., p. 410
Deep Creek Bridge.
Tarlton ffleming and Stephen Bedford Gent. are Appointed to view the Bridge over Deep Creek on the River road when finished & receive the same if done Workman like.

19 June 1744 O.S., p. 425
Road to be Cleard.
Ordered that the Male labouring Titheables belonging to the under mentioned persons do assist in Opening & clearing the Road for the first time from the three Chopt road to the Church of which John Hollow is Appointed Overseer Viz^t. Thos. Cauthon Overseer for Michael Holland Pouncy Anderson James Graves Overseer for John Smith Thos. Sanders James ffarguson Philip Hoggatt ffra^s. Kerby Henry Wood Henry Martin Henry Atkins William Dudgins Mich^l. Holland Junr. John Sandland Benjamin Henson John Kid William Gardner Edm^d. Hodges Edward Houchins John Houchins James Alford Capt. Holland Henry Parish & John Witt.

19 June 1744 O.S., p. 434
Deep Creek Bridge.
The Bridge built over Deep Creek by ffrancis James is received and Thomas Turpin Gent. late Sherif is directed to Pay him twenty pounds

Curr^t. money for the same and Ten pounds Curr^t. money for building the Stocks and Pillory if so much is in his hands.

20 Aug. 1744 O.S., p. 477
Court for Proof of Publick Claims
Petition for Two fferrys over the North River is read and ordered to be Certified to the General Assembly.

A Petition for fferry at Ashford Hughes's is read and ordered to be Certified to the General Assembly.

21 Aug. 1744 O.S., p. 488
Lickinghole Bridge.
Ordered that the Three Gangs nearest to Little Lickinghole Bridge do meet and make a Bridge and Causway and Samuel Ridgway is Appointed Overseer

18 Sept. 1744 O.S., p. 491
Surveyor of Road
John Mosely is Appointed Surveyor of the road in the room of Henry Clay.

Thomas Jones is Appointed Surveyor of the road from Tye River to ffendlys Gap and from thence the nearest way to the South River.

Ordered that the Titheables on Tye River, Mason[?] and Capt James Nevils,s do Clear the same.

18 Sept. 1744 O.S., p. 498
Road to be Viewed.
Ordered that Chas. Anderson James Brown & Obediah Woodson do view the Road going by Edward Davisons Plantation and make report thereof to the Court.

20 Nov. 1744 O.S., p. 508
Surveyor of Road.
Benjamin Cocke is Appointed Surveyor of the road from Pleasants Beverdam Bridge to Little Lickinghole.

Ordered that all the Titheables on the North side the River road above Lickinghole except John Smiths and M^r. Massies lower Quarter be added to M^r. Hopkins's Gang.

John Massie is Appointed Surveyor of the road in the room of William Walton.

George Payne Junr. is Appointed Surveyor of Paynes road in the room of James Hopper and that the said Harper be added to M^r. Hopkin's Gang.

Thomas Morrison is Appointed Surveyor of the Road from the halfway run to Capt. Charles Lynchs Bridge.

James Martin is Appointed Surveyor of the road from Capt. Charles Lynchs Bridge to Whitesidess Creek.

John Dobbins is Appointed Surveyor of the Road from Whitesides's Creek to Woods's ffield

John McCord is Appointed Surveyor of the Road from Woods's ffield to the D. S. Tree.

15 January 1744 O.S., p. 535
Surveyor of Road.
Arthur Mosely is Appointed Surveyor of the road in the room of George Williamson.

Isaac Allen is Appointed Surveyor of the road in the room of Richard Ward and John Bostick.

15 January 1744 O.S., p. 535
Surveyor of Road.
Benjamin Harrison is Appointed Surveyor of the middle road from Willis's River to Albemarl County line.

Joseph Price is Appointed Surveyor of the River road from Willis's River Bridge to Albemarl County line.

15 Jan. 1744 O.S., p. 543
Road to be Cleared.
Ordered that a Road be Cleared from Solomon's Creek road into the Chapple road and that Joell Chandler be Surveyor thereof

Ordered that Bartholomew Stovall Joell Chandler's Sons and Edmund Toney do Clear the said road.

19 Feb. 1744 O.S., p. 544
Road to be Cleared.
Ordered that Joseph Pace and his Gang do open a road from the Main road of which he is Surveyor to M^r. Benjamin Cocke's fferry

ADDENDUM

Additional County Levy Information

A number of transportation-related entries from the Goochland County levies were omitted from the original published volume. These are included below.

1 October 1729, O. S., Book 1, p. 156
County levy
To Sarah Atkinson for keeping fferry from May Court after the rate of 800 lb Tobacco
P. Annum   301 [pounds of tobacco]

17 September 1730, O.S., Book 2, p. 47
County levy
to [torn: Ste?]phen Hughes for keeping fferry from May Court till this [torn] after the rate of fifteen hundred pounds of tob^o P^r. Annum   625 [pounds of tobacco]

Edward Williams Gent. to enable him to pay ffrances Jam[torn: probably James] and John Harris this County's proportion of tobacco for building the bridge over Tuckahoe Creek
                                                                      6000 [pounds of tobacco]

7 October 1732, O. S., Book 3, p. 118
County levy
To Stephen Hughes for keeping fferry one year ending September 17
                                                                      2377 [pounds of tobacco]

9 October 1733, O. S., Book 3, p. 215
County levy
To Stephen Hughes for keeping fferry   1600 [pounds of tobacco]
                                                                      64 Cask

(p. 217)
To Joseph Dabbs for fferriages &^{c}.   £1.3.0

16 October 1734, O. S., Book 3, p. 307
County levy
To Stephen Hughes for keeping fferry   1600 [pounds of tobacco]
                                                                      64 Cask

To Stephen Hughes for the ferryman's levey last year   20 [pounds of tobacco]

10 Oct. 1737 O.S., Book 4, p. 249
County Levy
To Isham Randolph towards Bridges   4000 [pounds of tobacco]

17 December 1739 O.S., Book 4, p. 446
County Levy
To Jacob Michaux for fferrying at the Election   100 [pounds of tobacco]

17 November 1740, O. S., Book 4, p. 512
County levy
To Robert Atkinson for keeping fferry one year   1600 [pounds of tobacco]
                                                 64 Cask

28 November 1741, O. S., Book 5, p. 15
County levy
To Robert Atkinson's widow for keeping fferry one year   800 [pounds of tobacco]
                                                         32 Cask

To Jacob Michaux for keeping fferry one year   800 [pounds of tobacco]
                                                 32 Cask

18 October 1742, O. S., Book 5, p. 154
County levy
To Robert Atkinson's widow for keeping fferry   800 [pounds of tobacco]
                                                  32 Cask

To Jacob Michaux for keeping D°   800 [pounds of tobacco]
                                                 32 Cask

INDEX - GOOCHLAND COUNTY ROAD ORDERS

Note: This index is arranged by subject: Personal Names; Bridges; Chapels, Churches and Glebes; Fords; County Government; Ferries; Houses; Mills; Mountains, Ridges, Thoroughfares and Gaps; Plantations; Quarters; Rivers, Creeks, Branches, Swamps, Slashes, Springs; Roads; Signposts, Markers, Direction Stones, etc.; Road Surveyors Gangs; Miscellaneous

Personal Names:
Ebenezer Adams, 8
Robert Adams, 18, 44
Henry Adkins (Atkins), 7
John Alexander, 49
James Alford, 53
Benjamin Allen, 12
Charles Allen (Allin), 34, 37, 53
Isaac Allen, 55
Samuel Allen (Allin), 25, 41, 48
Samuel Allen Junr., 26, 31
William Allen (Allin), 17, 25, 29, 31[2], 38
Charles Anderson, 36, 48, 51, 54
Henry Anderson, 14
Pouncy Anderson, 53
John Anthony, 33
Joseph Anthony, 39
Thomas Applebury, 17
James Armour, 41
Saml. Arnett, 41
Samuel Arnold, 44, 52
John Arthers, 36
Henry Atkins, 53
Robert Atkinson, 57
Robert Atkinson's widow, 57[2]
Sarah Atkinson, 5, 6, 7, 56
Willm. Atkinson Junr., 33
William Bailey, 33
Henry Baily, 41
Thomas Baily, 33
ffras. Baker, 33
Leonard Ballew's, 27
Lilliard Ballew, 5
Thomas Ballew, 43[2], 52[2]
James Barnes, 35, 41
John Barnet (Barnit), 34[2]
Capt. Barnets', 41
Mr. Barrets, 47
Joseph Barringer, 16, 17, 36

Barringers' (Barrengers) 22, 42[2]
William Bass 49
Nathaniel Basset, 5, 6, 17
Isaac Bates, 51
John Bates's, 50
William Battersby, 28
John Baugh, 26
Joseph Baugh, 23, 28, 51
Stephen Bedford, 43, 44, 49[2], 50, 53
Capt. Bedford, 47
James Bell, 39, 41
James Bell, Junr., 41
Samuel Bell, 39, 41
Thomas Bell, 41
Anthony Bennin (Bening), 16, 38, 40, 41
Joseph Bening, 38
Robert Berherd, 38
John Bibe, 35, 46
Thomas Bibe, 33
John Bide, 42
widow Blackburn's, 13
Joseph Bingley, 33, 35, 37, 42
Archibald Blake, 53
Thomas Boesand, 14
Major Bolling's, 5, 6[2], 7, 35[2], 36, 46
Edward Booker, 43, 44
John Bostick 8, 14, 23, 34, 55
Benjamin Bradshaw, 27, 37, 45, 48
Danl. Brits, 21
Peter Brooks, 36
James Brown, 48, 54
James Bryan, 42
Charles Burk 53
Samuel Burk, 13, 17[2]
William Burk, 50, 51
Hutchins Burton, 14
Norvel (Nowel) Burton, 26, 34[2], 38, 41, 48
Richard Burton, 38, 41
Robert Burton, 7
Edmund Butler, 17, 24
Samuel Butler 6, 7
William Cabell, 9, 13, 22, 43, 51
Chas. Caffrey, 41
John Cannon, 38, 52
George Carrington, 21, 22, 25, 28, 30[2], 33, 44, 49
Edward Carter, 38
Honble John Carter Esqr., 42

Robert Carter, 22
Thomas Carter 47
Henry Cary, 8, 24, 28, 32, 35, 36$^{(2)}$
James Cary, 36
Joseph Cary, 36
Miles Cary, 23
Howard Cash, 41, 44
Thomas Cawthorn (Cauthon), 17, 53
Gideon Chambon, 11, 12$^{(2)}$
William Chamberlaine, 10
Joel Chandler, 11, 40, 55$^{(2)}$
Joell Chandler's Sons, 55
William Chandler, 11
Peter Chastain, 38, 41
Stephen Chastain, 5, 7
Abraham Childers, 52
Henry Chiles, 34
Jas. Christian, 42
Robert Christian, 33
Thos. Christian, 38
Widow Christian, 33
David Clarkson, 6, 7
Henry Clay, 24, 26$^{(2)}$, 54
William Clay, 26
John Cobb, 28
Benjamin Cocke, 44, 45, 51, 54, 55
James Cock, 11
Richard Cocke, 7
Jno. Cocks, 38
James Code, 14
Mathew Collins, 7
Bryan Conolly, 36
William Cook, 36
Abraham Cowley, 28
ffrederick Cox, 11, 37, 41
John Cox, 11, 17, 38
Mathew Cox, 5$^{(2)}$
Nicholas Cox, 5, 9, 14$^{(2)}$, 15, 17, 25
Stephen Cox, 12, 14, 15, 49
Richard Crouch, 49
Edward Curd, 7
John Curds, 35$^{(2)}$, 42
Curds, 36
Joseph Dabbs, 47, 48, 56
James Daben, 39
John Daben, 39
James Daniel, 45, 48, 52

Nicholas Davies, 40, 50, 51
David Davis, 16, 19
Robert Davis, 20, 33
William Davis, 11
Edward Davisons, 54
Hugh Dennum, 53
John Denny, 36
Thomas Dickins, 11, 13, 16, 19
Dudley Digges 8, 23, 35
Hugh Dobbins, 41
Hum Dobbins, 41
John Dobbins, 41, 55
Thomas Dobbins, 41
Dennis Doyle, 41
William Dudgins, 53
Martin Dunken(Dunkin), 8, 16, 22
John Dunn, 13
Robt. Dute, 36
Warham Easly, 7
William Easly, 11, 36
Thomas Edwards, 24, 31
John Edmunds, 14
ffrances Epes, 14
Collo. Eppes's, 24[(2)]
James ffarguson, 53
John ffarrar, 34
Joseph.ffarrar, 13[(2)], 34, 44
James ffendly, 48, 53[(2)]
James ffidler, 41
John ffleming, 13, 25, 38, 43, 51, 56
Tarlton ffleming, 5, 16, 23, 25, 28, 30, 31[(2)], 36, 37, 38, 43, 47, 53
Majr. ffleming, 47
Ralph fflippen, 34
John fford's, 5, 6
John Franklin (ffranklin), 11, 17, 50
Hugh ffrazier, 41
James ffreeland, 53
John ffulton, 41
William Gardner, 53
James Gates's, 37
Doctr.Gays's 45
James Glen 36
Thomas Golsby, 6, 7
Claude Gorey, 11, 12[(2)], 16
Bennet Goods, 43, 45[(2)]
James Graves, 53
Nathl. Graves, 49

Ralph Graves, 42, 46[(2)], 49
mr. Graves, 44, 47
Willm. Grays, 36, 38
Mr. Grays, 36
David Griffin, 53
John Gunn, 27
William Halliday (holladay), 24, 37, 45
Theo. Hanks, 33
Thomas Harbour, 36, 50
Hardings, 13
William Hargis, 41
John Harmer, 36
Benjamin Harris, 50
John Harris 16, 37, 49, 56
William Harris, 30, 34
Benjamin Harrison, 8, 35, 41, 55
David Hattaway, 14
Benja. Hawkins, 36
Peter Hairston, 41
John Heard, 41
James Henderson, 41
Richard Henderson, 36
William Henderson, 33
James Hendlys, 43
John Henry, 42[(2)]
Benjamin Henson, 53
Edwin Hickman, 45, 53
Daniell Hix, 12
Marmaduke Hix, 9[(2)], 17
Edmd. Hodges, 53
Thos. Hodges, 36
John Hodnet, 36
Anthony Hoggatt, 5, 6, 13[(2)], 15, 17, 18, 19, 23, 24[(2)], 26, 28, 32, 48
Philip Hoggatt, 53
John Holland, 52
Michael Holland, 53
Michl. Holland. Junr., 53
Capt. Holland, 53
John Hollow, 53
James Holman, 13, 44, 46
Arthur Hopkins, 22[(2)], 27[(2)], 46[(2)], 57
Doctor Hopkins, 28
Mr. Hopkins, 36, 54
James Hopper, 53, 54
Edward Houchins, 53
John Houchins, 53
Allen Howard, 5, 6, 7, 14[(2)], 17, 19[(2)], 33[(2)], 37

Charles Hudson 22
Anthony Hughes, 11, 37, 41, 48
Ashford Hughes's, 54
Charles Hughes, 41
Isaac Hughes, 11
Robert Hughes, 44, 46, 47, 50
Stephen Hughes, 6, 7, $9^{(2)}$, 14, $15^{(2)}$, $17^{(2)}$, 43, 45, $56^{(5)}$
Thomas Hughes, 41
Jos: Hunter, 38
Strangeman Hutchens, 34
John Isham, 53
Joseph Jackson, 9, 47
ffrancis James 17, 24, $37^{(2)}$, 38, 39, 43, 45, 50, 53, 56
Peter Jefferson, 20, $21^{(2)}$, 22, 25, 27, 28, 33, $36^{(2)}$, $44^{(2)}$
Saml. Jemison, 41
John Jemison, 41
Joseph John, 11
Daniel Johnson, 11, 50
Henry Johnson, 53
Isaac Johnson, 34
James Johnson, 48
John Johnson, 34
Sarah Johnson's, 26
widow Johnson's, 21
John Jones, 44
Thomas Jones, 44, 48, 53, 54
Thomas Joplin, 7, 34
Chas. Jordan, 40, 46
Robt. Kent, 33
William Kent, 36
ffras. Kerby, 53
John Kid 53
Martin King $8^{(2)}$, 44
James Kinkead, 41
William Knight's, 19
John Laine, 8, 21, 42
Thomas Lawhan 12
Jonas Lawson's, 28
Timothy Lee, 14
Lee (Overseer), 29
Charles Lewis, 31, 36
David Lewis, 41, 50
David Lewis, Junr., 41
John Lewis, 12
Robert Lewis' s, 33
William Lewis, 41
Major Lewis, 53

Thomas Locket, 23
David Lyles's, 21
Charles Lynch, 20, 27, 32, 36, 44, 45, 49, 55[(2)]
Meridith Manning, 38, 41
David Martin, 41
Henry Martin, 50, 53
James Martin, 39, 44, 52, 55
Peter Martin, 32, 42
Thomas Martin, 44
Willm. Martin, 33
Collo. Martins, 36
Alexander Marshall, 36
Charles Massie, 33
John Massie, 54
Capt. Massies, 28
Mr. Massies, 54
Edwd. Maxeys, 37
Silvanus Maxey, 37, 53
William May, 7, 10, 36
Joseph Mayo, 7
William Mayo, 5, 6, 8, 14[(2)], 16, 26, 29, 49
Major Mayo's, 26
John Mackbride (McBride), 5, 10, 12, 24
John McCord, 39, 4l, 55
William McCoy, l4
Robert McNeely, 41
Andrew McWilliams, 41
William Megginson, 39
Edward M'gehe, 36
Jacob Micheaux (Michaux), 5, 6, 11, 24[(2)], 25, 26, 27, 45, 48, 50, 51, 53, 57[(3)]
Paul Micheaux (Michaux), 11, 43, 45[(4)], 46, 50[(2)]
William Miller, 41
William Mills, 36
Edward Molloy, 41
John Moor, 7
Thomas Moor, 26
William Moor, 7
Andrew Moreman, 32
Anthony Morgan, 11, 45
Thos. Morrison, 39, 41, 55
William Morrison, 41
Morrisons, 39, 44
Joseph Morton, Junr., 18
Benjamin Moseby (Mosby), 17, 20, 39, 42
Hezekiah Mosby, 48
Jacob Mosby, 47
John Mosby, 22

Richard Moseby (Mosby), 15, 25, 26, 39, 43, 48
Capt. Mosby's, 47
Arthur Mosely, 55
John Mosely, 54
Capt. Moseley's, 26
James Moss, 6, 7
John Moss, 33
William Moss, 47
John Mossoms, 52, 53[(2)]
Patrick Mullin, 14, 17
Thomas Murrels', 6, 15
John Netherland, 24, 25[(2)], 26
Wade Netherland, 43, 47
James Nevill 8, 44, 54
John Nichols, 47
James Nowlin, 5, 10, 35, 36, 45
John Owen, 51, 52
William Owen's, 8
all the Owens, 33
John Ownby, 36
Joseph Pace, 36, 37, 45, 55
John Pankey, 28
Henry Parish, 53
Richard Parkers', 5, 7[(2)], 14, 18, 19, 24, 48
Thomas Parker, 30
David Patteson, 33
George Payne, 5, 9, 13, 18, 19, 23
George Payne Junr., 54
John Payne, 34, 36, 38, 51
Josiah (Josias) Payne, 19, 27, 53
Robert Peak, 36
Abraham Perkins, 7
Constant Perkins, 6, 13
William Pirkins (Perkins), 43, 52
George Perrin, 7
Thomas Pleasants, 25, 36, 39
Pleasants, 45, 54
John Pollock, 35, 37
Anthony Pouncy, 40
John Povals, 52
Geo: Powel, 41
Uriah Print, 41
John Prior, 8[(3)], 36
Sylvester Prophet, 22
Thomas Prosser, Attorney, 19
Andrew Pruit, 6
John Quin, 5[(2)]

John Radford, 37
William Radford, 45
George Raine, 13
Beverly Randolph's, 34, 37
Isham Randolph, 9[(2)], 22, 23, 25, 31[(3)], 32, 40, 45, 47, 57
(Collo.) Richard Randolph, 7, 24, 26, 32, 47
Thomas Randolph, 12
William Randolph, 23[(2)], 30[(3)], 32, 35, 38, 45, 46, 52
William Randolph Junr., 17, 20, 39, 52
Honble. William Randolph Esqr., 40
Honble. William Randolph Esqr., deced, 49
Colo. Randolph's, 29
Mr. Randolph, 35
Mrs. Randolph, 47, 49
David Rees, 41
Alexander Reid, 41
John Reid, 39
John Richards, 22
John Richardson, 10, 38, 42, 46, 47
Samuel Ridgway, 45, 54
John Rights (Wright), 8[(2)], 38
John Ripley, 14[(2)]
John Roberts, 41, 47
William Roberts's, 48
James Robertson, 41
James Robinson, 39
John Robinson, 32
Robt. Rogers's, 35
Henry Runnals, 18, 20
William Sallee, 19, 38
William Sampson, 49
Rbbert Sanders, 40, 41, 45
Stephen Sanders, 51
Thomas Sanders, 51, 53
John Sandland, 53
John Saunders', 5, 20, 25
Thomas Saunders, 15[(2)], 19
John Hyde Saunders, 25, 29, 45, 48
Ann Scott, 35
Edward Scott, 9, 10[(5)], 11, 12, 19, 21, 25, 27[(3)], 31
Joseph Scott, 38
Samuel Scott, 43, 49
Mr. Scott, 26
Scotts, 42
Scruggs (Overseer), 29
James Sheltons, 28
Mr. Shelton, 16

James Skelton, 17
Abraham Slater, 41
John Small, 39
Lazarus Small, 39
John Smith, 47, 48, 53, 54
Thomas Smith's, 33
Mr. Smith 33
John James Solager, 38
John Sorrell, 7
George Southerland, 22
James Spears, 13$^{(2)}$, 17
James Spencer, 52
Samuell Spencer, 11, 52
Charles Spurlock, 10, 36
Samuel Stephens, 53
Samuel Stiles, 41
Alexander Stinson, 36
Davis Stockdon, 41, 44$^{(2)}$
Richard Stockdon, 41
Thomas Stockdon, 41
Young Stokes, 14, 43, 49
Daniel Stoner, 6, 11, 14, 15$^{(2)}$, 16$^{(2)}$, 21, 25, 30, 32, 38
Thomas Stones, 28
Bartholomew Stoval, 11, 55
George Stoveall, 5$^{(2)}$, 9, 28, 41
Peter Sublett, 19
Edwd. Tanner, 37$^{(2)}$
Charles Taylor, 32
George Taylor, 41
John Taylor 29$^{(2)}$
James Terry, 48
Joseph Thomas, 5
Philip Thomas, 7, 14, 29
George Thompson, 6, 7
James Thompson, 14
Robert Thompson, 49, 51
Edmund Toney, 55
David Towns, 49
James Treland, 41
Alexander Trent, 41, 51
John Tuly, 14$^{(2)}$
Charles Turnbull, 46
Thomas Turpin, 11, 29, 31, 37, 38, 43, 53
John Twitty, 28
Samuel Vardry, 25
Abraham Venable, 33
William Verdeman, 39, 41

Autho. Vilen, 38
Richard Wade 13$^{(2)}$, 47
Thomas Wadlow, 7, 20
David Walker, 6, 7, 10, 12, 35, 37
John Walker, 33
Thomas Walker, 18
Andrew Wallace, 41
William Wallace, 41
William Walton, 48, 54
Richard Ward, 19, 42, 44, 55
William Wards, 47
Peter Ware, 25
James Watkins (Wodkins), 37, 38, 41
Joel Watkins, 34
Joseph Watkins, 7, 13, 20
John Watson, 34, 45
Watsons', 24
Thos.Watts, 53
John Weads, 39
Henry Webbs, 28
John Webb, 5, 12, 20$^{(2)}$, 34
Philip Webber, 16, 21, 34
Thomas Wharton, 22
Benjamin Wheeler, 28, 32, 33, 44
William Wheeler, 14
John White, 30, 39
Samuel White, 14
William White, 41
John Williams, 37, 42
William Williams, 35, 37, 41
George Williamson, 34, 37, 49$^{(2)}$, 55
Robert Willis Junr., 47
Willis's, 52
Nicholas Wilkinson, 11
Israel Winfry, 51
Jacob Winfrey 17, 18, 41
Benjamin Witt 38, 41
John Witt, 40, 47, 53
William Witts 44
William Womack (Wamack), 5$^{(2)}$, 12, 18, 22, 29, 42
William Womack Junr. 32, 36
Henry Wood, 6, 7$^{(2)}$, 10, 13$^{(2)}$, 17, 23, 36, 53
Edward Wood, 8
Archibald Woods, 41
John Wood(s), 12, 41
Michael Wood(s), 28, 41$^{(2)}$
Michael Woods Junr., 41

William Woods, 41
Wood's, 55[2]
John Woodson, 7, 14, 15[3], 21, 33
Joseph Woodson, 7, 11, 12, 14, 19, 23, 24, 29, 38, 43
Josiah Woodson, 12
Obediah Woodson, 39, 51, 54
Sanburn Woodson 45[2]
Stephen Woodson, 12, 14, 25
Tarlton Woodson, 21
Tarlton Woodson Junr., 40
Tucker Woodson, 43, 44, 46, 50[2]
William Woodson, 50
John Woody, 32, 33
Thomas Wooldridge, 28
John Worley 23[2], 26
John Wright (Right), 31, 33

Bridges:
Appomattox River Bridge, 38, 43, 44, 49
old Bridge near Majr. Bollings mill, 36
Back Road Bridge, 5
Beverdam Creek Bridge, 5, 8[3], 10[2], 15, 16, 19, 21, 25, 33, 36, 39, 40, 54
Bird Creek Bridge, 28, 30, 31, 36
Burton's Bridge, 48
County bridge, 12
Curds Bridge, 38
Deep Creek bridge, 15, 16, 20, 21, 24, 25, 26, 27, 28[2], 29, 35, 42[2], 46, 49, 51, 53[2]
Dover Mill Creek Bridge, 25
ffine Creek bridge, 29
Great Guiney Creek Bridge, 34
Horseley's Bridge, 22,
Jones Creek bridge, 9, 16, 26, 32, 35, 37[2], 38, 40, 50
Little Creek bridge, 31
little licking hole Creek Bridge, 22, 27, 40, 54
Lickinghole Creek Bridge, 31
long branch Bridge, 31
Capt. Charles Lynchs Bridge, 55[2]
Moseby's bridge, 26
Muddy Creek bridge, 5, 21, 24, 25
My Chunk Creek Bridge, 36, 39[2]
Netherland's bridge, 26
Pleasants Beverdam Bridge, 54
lower Tuckahoe Creek Bridge, 21
Tuckahoe Creek Bridges, 5, 7, 13[2], 17, 23[2], 32, 34, 56
Willis's Bridge, 52
Willis's Creek Bridge, 28, 30[2], 31, 32, 33
Willis's River Bridge, 39, 40, 44, 48

Bridge Timber, 50
Causeways, 27, 38, 54

Chapels, Churches and Glebes:
Chappell, 11, 28, 35, 41, 42[2], 46, 52
Deep Creek Chapple, 46
Lickinghole Chapple, 43, 51
Church, 10, 12, 22, 46, 53
ffrench Church, 19
new Church, 12
the Glebe, 22, 42, 46
the Vestry, 22
King William Parish, 12

Fords:
Elk ford (on the Bird), 8[3]
horn Quarter fford, 40, 41
Lyles's fford, 21, 39, 40, 51, 52
Mount Misery fford, 14
Patricks fford, 5
Secretarys fford, 39, 41, 53

County Government:
Act of Assembly, 35
Albemarl County line, 55
Amelia County, 38, 49
Amelia County Court, 38, 43, 49
Constables, 46
Coroners, 46
County Levy Court, 37, 46, 50, 56, 57
County Line, 5[2], 6, 7, 13[2], 32, 35, 37
Court for Proof of Publick Claims, 54
Court days, 7
Court house, 6[3], 7[2], 12, 14, 15, 20[2], 21[2], 23, 24, 26, 29[3], 30, 35[3], 38
General Assembly, 54[2]
Goochland County Court, 46
Governor's Superseadee, 31
Grand Jury, 17, 19, 21, 23, 26, 31, 38, 46, 53
Guards, 46
Hanover County, 6, 37, 40
Henrico County Court, 32
Henrico County line, 23, 32, 34
Ordinary Lycenses
    Cox's, 38
    Michaux's, 27
    Parker's, 30
    Scots, 35

Taylors, 32
Prisoners, 46
Sherif, 7, 9, 46, 53
Stocks and Pillory, 54
Surveyor of Roads' fine, 17

Ferries:
Bennet Goods fferry 43, 45[(2)]
Mr. Benjamin Cocke's fferry, 55
County fferry, 6, 46
Court house Ferry, 6, 7, 9, 23, 26, 29
Dover fferry, 26
fferry at Elk Island, 43
James ffendly's fferry, 48, 53
fferry, 5, 6[(2)], 9, 10, 12[(2)], 21, 32, 38, 43, 47
fferry at Ashford Hughes's, 54
Manakin Town Ferry, 6[(2)], 14, 25, 29, 30, 32, 35, 38, 40, 46
Jacob Michaux's Ferry, 27
Michaux's Ferry, 27
fferry at Richard Mosebys to Tarlton fflemings, 43
Capt. Mosby's fferry, 47
Mosbys fferry, 47
Stephen Woodson deceas'd's fferry, 30
Tucker Woodson's fferry, 43, 44
Woodson's fferry, 25
Two fferrys over the North River, 54
fferry from the point of fork of James River to both sides of The River, 8
Paul Michaux's fferryboat, 46
fferry Keeper, 30, 35, 38
fferry Keepers levy, 50
fferry Keeper's payment, 9
Bennet Goods fferry Landing, 45[(2)]
Ferry landing, 5, 8[(2)], 12[(2)], 14, 15[(3)]
Mosbys fferry landing, 51
fferryman, 32
Petitions for ferries, 43[(5)], 54[(2)]
fferry rates, 6, 8
Paul Michaux's fferryboat, 46
fferry Keeper, 30, 35, 38
fferry Keepers levy, 50
fferry Keeper's payment, 9
Bennet Goods fferry Landing, 45[(2)]
Ferry landing, 5, 8[(2)], 12[(2)], 14, 15[(3)]
Mosbys fferry landing, 51
fferryman, 32
Petitions for ferries, 43[(5)], 54[(2)]
fferry rates, 6, 8

Houses:
Thomas Ballew's house, 43
Bates's House, 49[(2)], 53
Nowel Burton's house, 48
James Daniels' house, 48
Anthony Hoggatt's house, 48
William Megginson's house, 39
Jacob Mosby's house, 47
Wade Netherland's house, 47
William Randolph's dwelling house, 20
John Hyde Sander's house 48
John Smith's house, 47
Joseph Woodson's former dwelling house, 29
John Wright's house 32

Mills:
Major Bollings Mill, 5, 6[(2)], 7, 8, 19[(2)], 35, 36, 46
Floodgates, 35
Brooks's mill, 34, 36, 39
Dover mills, 15, 16, 21[(2)], 23, 25[(2)], 30, 40, 46, 50
Dover mill dam, 23
Hoggatts Mill, 24, 46
Alexander Marshall's Mill, 36
the Mill, 12
Secretarys mill, 40
Tuckahoe Creek mill, 6[(3)], 7, 10, 13, 20
Woodson's mill 5

Mountains, Ridges, Thoroughfares and Gaps:
Appamatox ridge, 6
Ward's Appamatox ridge, 5
Blew Ledge of Mountains, 28
ffendlys Gap, 51, 54
Hatchers Creek Mountains, 38
Little Mountains, 51
the Mountains 18[(2)], 19, 20, 33
ridge between the North River & Pamunkey River, 18
ridge between Deep Creek and Muddy Creek, 45
the Ridge, 36
Sclate River Mountain, 52
Thorrowfare, 39

Plantations:
John Alexander's Plantation, 49
Widow Atkinson's Plantation, 9
Leonard Ballew's upper Plantation, 27

Majr. Bolling's Plantation, 35
Buckingham Plantation, 8, 35, 38
Nowel Burton's Plantation, 34
Collo. John Carter's Plantation, 20
Clear Mount, 42
Mr. Richard Cocke's Plantation, 14
Edward Davison's Plantation, 54
Dudley Digges's Plantation, 24
Glovers Plantation, 52
Glovers old Plantation, 50, 52
Allen Howard's Plantation, 18, 19
Charles Hudson & others Plantations, 22
Plantation of Joseph Jackson, 9
Long Acre, 13
plantation belonging. to William Mayo, 8
Jacob Michaux's Plantation, 48
William Owen's Plantation, 8
Plantations on the River, 47
Thomas Pleasants' Plantation, 25
Anthony Pouncy's Plantation, 40
Mr. Beverly Randolphs Plantation, 34
Robert Sanders's old Plantation, 45
Mr. Edward Scott's Plantation, 14
John Smiths Plantation, 48
Thomas Smith's Plantation, 33
Thomas Walker's Plantation, 18
Richard Wards Plantation, 44
Richard Wards Plantation on Green Creek, 44
William Womack's Plantation, 18
John Wright's Plantation, 8

Quarters:
James Allens Qr., 36
John Arthers Qr., 36
Buffelo Quarter, 44
Mr. Henry Cary's upper Quarter, 24
Clear mount Quarters, 42
Doctr. Gays's Quarter, 45
Mr. Hopkins Quarter, 36, 50
horn Quarter, 40, 41
Robert Hughes' Quarter, 46
Jenito Quarter, 26
Letalone Quarter, 52
Chas. Lewis's mill Quarter, 36[(2)]
Mr. Massies lower Quarter, 54
Capt. Moseley's Quarter, 26
Pleasants Quarter, 45

Beverly Randolphs Quarter, 37
Collo. Richard Randolph's two upper Quarters, 24
Collo. Richard Randolph's two Quarters, 26
Colo. Randolph's two Quarters, 29
Mrs. Randolph's Quarter, 49
Secretary's Quarter, 22
Alexr. Trents Qr., 36
Tye River Quarters, 42
Watson's Quarter, 24[(2)]

Rivers, Creeks, Branches, Swamps, Slashes, Springs:
Clearing Rivers & Creeks, 46
Angola Creek, 48
    first Branch of, 19
    mouth of first branch of, 42
Appamatox River, 18, 29[(2)], 34[(3)], 37, 38, 39, 43, 44, 48, 49[(2)]
    fork of, 39
Appomattox River Banks, 29
Bamboo Creek, 33
Barringers Creek, 50[(2)]
Bear Creek, 24[(2)]
Bear Garden Creek, 33, 52
Beverdam, 5[(2)], 8, 10, 16, 21, 25, 33, 35[(2)], 36, 38, 39, 40, 46, 50, 54
Bird Creek 5[(2)], 14, 21[(3)], 22, 23[(2)], 28[(2)], 30, 31, 33, 36, 45, 48, 53
    mouth of, 16
    North Branch 8
    South branch 8[(2)]
Brooks's Spring, 37
Buck branch, 12[(2)], 23
Buck Island, 16, 17, 47
Butter Wood, 23
Carrols Creek, 33
branch above the Court house, 35
Deep Creek, 5[(2)], 9[(3)], 15, 16, 20, 21, 24, 26, 28[(2)], 29, 35, 41, 42, 45, 46[(2)], 47, 49, 51, 53
Ditoways (Dutoys) Branch, 26
    head of, 53
Dover Mill Creek, 25
Elk Island, 43
Elk lick, 8
ffine Creek, 5[(2)], 6[(2)], 7, 9, 11[(4)], 15, 16, 31, 37, 40, 42, 45[(2)], 49[(2)]
    ffork of, 11, 24
    North fork, 29
ffighting Creek, 46, 52
ffluvanna River, 52
genitoe (Jenetoe) Creek, 13, 23, 34
Georges Branch 52[(2)]
Green Creek, 42, 44, 48[(2)]

Great Guiney Creek, 34, 42$^{(2)}$
Little Guinea Creek, lower fork of, 14
halfway run, 55
Hardwarr River, 27, 44
    branches of, 30
    falls of, 30
Hatchers Creek, 38
horsepen branch, 47
Ivy Creek, 28
James River, 6$^{(2)}$, 8, 25
North branch of, 14
    North side of, 14, 28, 29$^{(2)}$, 45, 54
    point of fork, 8$^{(3)}$
    South side of, 5, 6, 8$^{(2)}$, 9, 32, 38, 45
Jones's Creek, 11$^{(2)}$, 16$^{(2)}$, 26, 32, 35, 37$^{(2)}$, 38$^{(2)}$, 40, 42, 49, 50
letalone Creek, 5, 7$^{(2)}$, 24, 53
    head of, 42
Little Creek, 21, 38
Licking hole Creek, 20, 31, 46$^{(2)}$, 54
    head of, 15, 19
    Upper ffork of, 53
Great Licking hole Creek, 8$^{(2)}$, 19, 22
little Licking hole Creek, 19, 22$^{(3)}$, 27, 31, 40, 54
long branch, 11$^{(2)}$, 31
lower Manakin Creek 7, 19, 50
Moors Creek, 50
Muddy Creek, 5$^{(3)}$, 9$^{(2)}$, 21$^{(2)}$, 22, 24, 34, 40, 45, 46
My Chunk Creek, 36$^{(2)}$, 39$^{(2)}$, 53
Negro Creek, fall on, 52
North River, 18, 27, 30, 33, 54
    ffork of, 22
    North side, 33
    South side, 22, 33
Northanna River,
    Northside of, 18
Pamunkey River, 18
Randolphs Creek, Head of, 38
Rivanna River, 8, 36, 42$^{(2)}$
    Crooked falls on, 36
    South side of, 36
the River, 24, 26, 47
    North side, 47
    South side, 47
Rock fish River, 14$^{(2)}$, 44$^{(2)}$
round pond, 22
Scicamore Island Creek, 52$^{(2)}$
Sclate (Slate) River, 27, 33$^{(2)}$, 43

       ffork of, 46
       Waltons ffork of, 47
Slash, 11$^{(2)}$
Solomon's Creek, 5$^{(2)}$, 6, 11, 31, 37, 50
Stony Creek, 5$^{(2)}$, 21
South River, 27, 51, 54
Thompsons branch, 52$^{(2)}$
Treasurer's Runn, 9
lower Tuckahoe Creek 21, 23
upper Tuckahoe Creek 21
Tuckahoe Creek, 5, 6$^{(2)}$, 7, 10, 17, 19, 32, 34, 56
Tye River, 33, 42, 44$^{(2)}$, 47, 51, 54$^{(2)}$
upper Creek, 11
Waltons ffork, 47
Webb's Spring, 22$^{(2)}$
Whitesides's Creek, 55$^{(2)}$
Wild Boar Swamp, 8
Willis's Creek, 5, 8$^{(2)}$, 21, 22, 28, 30$^{(2)}$, 31, 32, 33, 34
      Gravelly Fall of, 8
      South branch, 51
Willis's River, 38, 39, 40$^{(3)}$, 41, 44, 48$^{(2)}$, 55
      Head of, 32
Woodson's mill Creek, 5

Roads:

bridle way from John Alexander's Plantation into the River road near Mrs. Randolph's Quarter, 49

road from Angola Creek to Green Creek, 48

Back road, 5, 6$^{(3)}$, 12, 13

back road above Major Bolling's mill, 7

(road) from Bridge of the Said Back road untill it meets the river road, 5

Road from Leonard Ballews upper Plantation to slate River, 27

new road near Majr. Bollings mill to be discontinued, 36

old Road near Majr. Bolling's mill, 36

road from Bollings mill to Licking hole, 46$^{(2)}$

Barnets road, 40, 41, 46

road from Barnets road to horn Quarter fford on Willis River, 40

Road from Barnets road over Willis River at Horn Quarter fford to Glovers road, 41

Road from Barringers Creek to the Mountain Road, 50

Road from Bates's house to ffine Creek, 49

Road from Bear Creek to Watson's Quarter, 24

Road from Bear Garden Creek to Sclate River, 33

Bernard's road, 45, 48

Capt. Bernerds road, 38

Road from Beverdam Bridge to Bollings mill, 19

Road Beverdam Bridge to the branch above the Courthouse, 35

road from Bever dam bridge to Dover mill, 15, 21

Road from lower Beverdam Bridge to little licking hole Creek, 8

road from Beverdam Bridge to Martin Kings, 8

Road from Bever dam Bridge to Stony Creek, 21

(road) Beverdam Creek to Treasurer's Runn, 5

road from widow Blackburn's to the County line, 13

road from the Blew Ledge of Mountains to Ivy Creek, 28

Bradshaws road, 52

old road going by Bradshaws, 45

Road from Brooks mill to the fork of Appamatox River, 39

Road from Brooks's mill to his Land on Appamatox River, 34

Road from Brooks's mill to Arthers, 36

road from Buck branch to the County bridge, 12

road from Buck branch to the Mill, 12

Road from Buck Branch to Tuckahoe Bridge, 23

Buckingham Road, 32, 36, 45, 48[2], 52

Road from Buckingham downwards, 8

road from Buckingham road to Green Creek, 48

road from Buffelo Quarter to Tye River, 44

road Clear'd by Norvel Burton, 38

road from Nowel Burton's house over Willis's River at the Bridge built by the said Burton & Samuel Allin into Bernards road, 48

road from Nowel Burton's Plantation on Willis's Creek to a Plantation belonging to Mr. Dudley Digges called Buckingham, 34, 35

Road from the Bird to Danl. Brits, 21

road from about two miles above the mouth of the Bird Creek up the Country as far as Buck Island, 16

road from the Bird Creek to the North branch of James River at Mount Misery fford, 14

Road from the Bridge on the Bird Creek to the Crooked Falls on the Rivanna, 36

(road) from the Byrd to Patricks fford, 5

road from William Cabbell's house to Lickinghold Chapple, 43

road from William Cabbell's dwelling house into the main road, 13

road from John Carter's Tye River Quarters to his Clear mount Quarters, 42

Cary's path, 24

Road from Cary's path to Hoggatt's Mill, 24

Mr. Cary's road, 18[3], 29[2], 34

road between Mr. Cary's road and Appomattox River, 29

road from near the Chapple into the ffighting Creek road at or near the Negros Arm, 46

Road from the Chappel to the Upper Bridge on the main Deep Creek, 35

Chappel Road, 26, 28, 34, 37, 38, 40[3], 41[2], 42, 45, 48[2], 52, 55

road out of the Chapple road to extend along Capt. Bernerds road and from thence a Cross Willis's River near the road Clear'd by Norvel Burton to Buckingham & Crossing the Head of Randolphs Creek into Glovers road near to Hatchers Creek Mountains, 38

road from the Chapple road to Deep Creek Road, 41

road from near the Chappel road to Lyles's fford, 40

road along the Chapple road to Robert Sanders's old Plantation on Bernards road and from thence along the ridge between Deep Creek and Muddy Creek into Buckingham road, 45

Church road, 29, 48

Road from the County line in Lockets road to Appamatox River above Beverly Randolphs Quarter, 37

(road) from the County Line to fine Creek, 5

Court house Road, 21, 29

road between the two roads to the Court house, 35

road leading from the Court House to Appomattox River, 29

road from the Court house into the Back road above Major Bolling's mill, 6[(2)], 7

Road from the Court house to the Bird, 21

Road from the Courthouse to the fferry Landing, 12, 14, 15, 21, 38

road from the Court house (ffery) upwards into the main Road, 20[(2)], 23, 29

road from the Court house Ferry down the South side of the James River, 6

Road from the Court house towards Thomas Christian's, 24

Road from the Court house Road where it comes into the River road, to the ford at David Lyles's, 21

road which Nicholas Cox uses through the land of John Woodson, 15

road from the upper end of John Curds to the Lower end of Majr. Bolling's Plantation, 35

road from John Curds to Jas. Christians, 42

Road from the meadow above John Curds to the Court house, 35

Road below Curds, 36

road from Joseph Dabbs house into Collo. Richd. Randolphs road, 47

road to be cleared by Joseph Dabbs, 48

road from James Daniels' house to Willis's River on Buckingham road, 48

Road going by Edward Davisons Plantation, 54

Roads above & below Deep Creek, 20

road over Deep Creek, 15, 16

old road over Deep Creek in the Chapple, 41

(road) from Deep Creek to Muddy Creek, 5

road from Deep Creek Bridge to Barnets road, 46

road Deep Creek Bridge to Bates's House, 49

Road above Deep Creek Bridge on the Chappel Road to John Merrymans Path, 28

road from Deep Creek bridge to the Court house road, 29

road from Deep Creek Chapple to the ffork of Sclate River, 46

Deep Creek road, 40, 41

road from Thomas Dickins dwelling house to the main road, 11

Road from Dudley Digges's Plantation to Bear Creek, 24

Road from Ditoways Branch to Watkin's Path, 26

road from Dover fferry to the main Road on North side the River, 26

road from Dover mill to Beverdam, 46, 50

road from Dover mill to Beaverdam Bridge, 16, 25, 35, 40

road from Dover Mill to the Court House, 30

Road from the D. S. Tree down to Moors Creek and into the Secretarys Road, 50 road from the D. S. tree to Michael Woods, 41

Collo. Eppes's path, 24[(2)]

Road from Collo. Eppes's path to Let alone, 24

road from James ffendly's fferry to Thomas Jones's, 48, 53

bridleway from the fferry to the Church, 12

Road from the fferry to Jno. Cocks, 38

Road from the fferry to Jones's Creek Bridge and from the Bridge to the County line, 32

(road) from the ffery to the main road upwards, 6, 12, 21

road to the fferry landing, 51

road from ferry landing through low ground of Jacob Michaux for the upper and lower Inhabitants on South Side James River, 5

Road from the fferry landing opposite point of fork to main road, 8

road from fferry landing opposite the point of fork to the River Road, 8

new road from fferry landing to back road on the hills at Manacanton, 12

road from the fork of the fferry road upwards into the main road, 11

Road from ffine Creek to the County line below lower Manakin Creek, 7

Road from the upper branch of ffine Creek across the fork of Deep Creek thence up the ridge between Deep Creek and Muddy Creek, 9

road from ffine Creek to the fferry landing, 5

road from ffine Creek to Jones's Creek, 16, 49

Road from the ffork of ffine Creek to Jacob Michaux's Road, 24

(road) from fine Creek to Solomon's Creek, 5, 6, 11

where the roads meet just above fine Creek on Stephen Hughes's road, 45

ffighting Creek road, 46

Bridle Road from Ralph Flippens house and Muddy Creek into the Chappel road, 34 road from John ffords towards Appamatox ridge to be continued over both branches ffine Creek, 6

road from John fford's to Ward's Appamatox ridge, 5

road from genitoe Creek on the back road into Hoggats road, 13

Road from Georges Brance to or near Scicamore Island Creek, 52

road going from the Gleeb to the Church, 46

Road from the Glebe into the River Road towards the Church, 22

road from Glovers Plantation so farr 'till he meets Thomas Ballew, 52

River Road from Glovers old Plantation upwards, 50

road from Glovers old Plantation above Willis's to Georges Branch, 52

Glovers road, 38, 41, 47

road from Bennet Goods fferry Landing on the North side James River into the main road, 45

road from Bennet Goods fferry Landing on the South side James River into the main road, 45

road from Claude Gorey's into the road going to the bridge over Jones's Creek, 16

Road going through Ralph Graves' land to the Glebe, 42

old road and the new road Clear'd by mr Graves, 44

road from Great Guiney Creek to the mouth of the first branch of Angola Creek, 42

Road from Great Guiney Creek to Carys Road, 34

road from the falls of Hardwar to the north river, 30

Road from Henrico line over Butter wood to Jenitoe, 23

road from Anthony Hoggatts' house on Appamatox River into the road to be cleared by Joseph Dabbs, 48

Hoggats road, 13

road from James Holman's dwelling house into the main road, 13

Road from Mr. Hopkins Quarter to Barringers Creek, 50

Road from Mr. Hopkins Quarter up the Ridge to My Chunk Creek, 36

bridle way near Horn quarter, 18

Road from Horseley's Bridge to the new Bridge at little licking hole Creek, 22

Road from a little above Allen Howard's towards Brook's Spring in Hanover County, 37

road to pass near the Plantation of Allen Howard, 19

road to pass through Allen Howard's Plantation, 18

road from Robert Hughes' Quarter at Muddy Creek into the main road, 46

road between Robert Hughes & John Nichols, 47

Stephen Hughes's road, 45

main road on the North side of James River, 14

Road on the South side of James River leading towards the Head of Willis's River, 32

Road on the South side of James River, 38

Road of which Peter Jefferson is Surveyor, 22

Road from Jenetoe Creek to Appamatox River above Mr. Beverley Randolph's Plantation, 34

Jenetoe road, 49

Road from the widow Johnson's to the upper Tuckahoe Creek, 21

road from Jones Creek to fine Creek, 42

road from Jones's Creek Bridge to the County line, 35

road from Jones Creek bridge to ffine Creek, 40

Road from Jones's Creek Bridge to the Lower Manakin Creek, 50

road going to the bridge over Jones's Creek 16

Road from the ffork of the Road between Jones's Creek and fine Creek over the long branch, 11

road from Martin Kings to the Mountain ridge road, 44

road from the head of Letalone into the Chapple road near the Chapple, 42

Road from the Upper ffork of Licking Hole to the Little Byrd, 53

road between little Licking hole & great Licking hole Creeks, 19

road from little licking hole to great licking hole, 22

Road from Little Licking hole to Webb's Spring, 22

Road from Lickinghole Chapple into the Mountain road between Number thirty and thirty two, 43

Road from Lickinghold Chapple into the Mountain Road, 51

Road from Little Creek to Beverdam, 38

Road from Little Creek to the Bird, 21

Lockets road, 37

Road from the long branch _____ between Jones's Creek and fine Creek upwards as farr as cross the ffork ffine Creek, 11

Liles's road, 48[(2)]

road to Lyles's fford, 51

road from Lyles's fford to the Chapple road, 52

road from Lyles's fford laying between the Chapple road and Deep Creek road, 40

Road from the halfway run to Capt. Charles Lynchs Bridge, 55

road from Capt. Charles Lynchs Bridge to Whitesides Creek, 55

main road, 6[(2)], 8, 9, 11[(2)], 12, 20[(3)], 21, 23, 29[(2)], 43[(2)], 45[(3)], 46, 47[(3)], 55

road from the Main road of which he is Surveyor to Mr. Benjamin Cocke's ffery, 55

Lower main road to the Manacan Town fferry, 40

main Road on North Side the River, 26

bridle way from lower Manakin Creek to the ffrench Church, 19

Manakin Town road, 5, 7[(2)], 10, 11, 12[(2)], 15, 16[(2)], 17, 31 road from the Manakin town fferry to the main road on the North side of James River, 14, 29

Road from Alexander Marshalls Mill into Skin Quarter road, and into Buckingham road, 36

Majr. Mayos road, 37

Road from Major Mayo's to the ridge Road, 26

Bridle way from where Majr. Mayos road turns into the Chappel road to go by James Gate's, 37

John Merrymans path, 28

road from Jacob Michaux's to the Bates's house, 53

road from Jacob Michauxs Plantation to fall into the Church road between William Roberts's and Hezekiah Mosby, 48

Jacob Michaux's Road, 24

road from Paul Michaux to where the roads meet just above fine Creek on Stephen Hughes's road, 45

new part of the road from Paul Michaux to the fork of the road, 45

a new road from Paul Michaux into the main road going down the Country to fall into the main road below Stephen Hughes, 43

road from Paul Michaux to John Hide Sanders's, 45

middle road, 10, 45

mill dam, 23

road from mount Misery to the Bird, 23

road from Mount Misery fford to Rock fish River, 14

road from Morrison's to Davis Stockdons, 44

road from Thomas Morrisons to the D.S. Tree in Michael Woods road, 41

bridle path from Jacob Mosby's house between Deep Creek and horsepen branch into the main road, 47

road near Richard Mosby's Plantation, 15

Road from Mosbys fferry on the North side the River to Collo. Isham Randolphs, 47

road from Capt. Mosby's fferry on the South side the River to the main road, 47

road from John Mossoms to the Head of Dutoys branch, 53

Road from John Mossom to Lettalone, 53

Mountain road, 27, 28, 30, 32, 33, 42$^{(2)}$, 43, 44, 50, 51

Mountain ridge road, 44

(Mountain road) Road from a little below Number thirty six to his (John Wright's) house, 32

Bridle road from Mountain road to Barrengers on the Rivanna, 42$^{(2)}$

Road from the Mountains to the head of Licking hole 19, 20

Road from the Mountains down the Country on the Northside of the Northanna to meet Sander's Road, 18

road from the Mountains down the ridge between the North River & Pamunkey River, 18

road from Muddy Creek to Willis's Creek, 5, 21, 22

road from Muddy Creek on the River road to Willis's River Bridge, 40

road from Thomas Murrel's to the back road, 6

road from Thomas Murrell's towards the head of Licking hole Creek, 15

Road from My Chunk Creek to the Secretary's fford, 53

Napier's path, 24

road from John Netherlands' House to the main road 24

road from Wade Netherlands' house to the fferry, 47

Road from the North River up the ffork and Across Hardwarr River, 27

road of James Nowling to the floodgates of Majr. Bolling's mill, 35

Road from the Old Ordinary to the Bridge at long branch, 31

road from the Ordinary to the North fork of ffine Creek, 29

road from Richard Parker's to the first Branch of Angola, 19 road from near Richard Parker's to the upper inhabitants on Appamatox River, 18

road from Richard Parker's on letalone Creek the best way down to Manakin Town road, 5, 7[(2)]

Paynes road, 54

Road of Thomas Pleasants at Thomas Pleasant's Plantation, 25

road from Pleasants Beverdam Bridge to Little Lickinghole, 54

road the old way through Anthony Pouncy's Plantation which led into Hanover, 40

Raines road, 45

Road from Isham Randolphs above Treasurer's Runn into the main Road, 9

Colo. Richard Randolph's road, 32, 47

Colo. Randolph's Charriot road, 48

Road from Wm. Randolph's dwelling house to Tuckahoe Mill, 20

road from opposite Wm. Randolph's landing into the main Manacan Town Road, 17

ridge Road, 26

Road from John Rights down to Cords Bridge, 38

Path down the River from Buck Island to John Witts, 47

Road from the River to Napier's path, 24

main river road, 7

River road, 5[(3)], 8, 9, 10, 13, 16, 21, 22, 26, 30, 40, 49, 53

River road from the Byrd to John Smiths Plantation, 48

River road which passes through Anthony Bennins land, 16

River road from the County Line on the South Side James River to the Pit, 5

(road) from the river road up the Back road to the Bridge over Beverdam Creek below Major Bollings Mill, 5

road from the River road down to Sarah Johnson's, 26

John Robinson's path, 32

Road from John Robinsons path to Buckingham Road where Colo. Richard Randolph's road turns out, 32

road from Rock fish to Hardwar River, 44

Round Pond Road, 20

Road from the Round pond Road to Collo. John Carter's Plantation, 20

Road from the round pond to the Secretary's Quarter, 22

road from near John Hyde Sanders' house to Cross the Chapple road and fall into Liles's road or Collo. Randolphs Charriot road, 49

Saunder's Road, 18

Road from Scicamore Island Creek and to fall on Negro Creek between Sclate River Mountain and the ffluvanna, 52

road from Sclate River Opposite to Thomas Ballew's house, 43

Road from Sclate River upwards, 33

road from the Secretarys fford to the D.S. tree, 41

road from the Secretarys mill to the Lower main road to the Manacan Town fferry, 40

Secretarys Road, 50

Secretarys road to be continued from Tye River to ffendlys Gap on the Little Mountains and on to South River, 33, 51

Skin Quarter road, 36

road from the Slash on the upper side of the upper branch of ffine Creek to the Chappell, 11

road from John Smith's house to William Wards, 47

road going thro: Thomas Smith's Plantation at the Mountains, 33

Solomon's Creek road, 55

Road from Solomon's Creek road into the Chapple road, 55

(road) from Solomons Creek to Deep Creek, 5

Road from Solomons Creek to byne Creek, 31, 37

Stephens road, 13

road from Davis Stockdon's to D.S. tree, 44

Majr. Stoner's Road, 39

Road from Majr. Stoner's Road to Lyles's fford on Appamatox River, 39

(road) Stony Creek to Beverdam Creek, 5

road passing by the plantation of John Taylor, 29

Road from the Thorrowfare a little above Morrisons to the Secretarys fford, 39

road from Thompson's branch to Bear Garden Creek, 52

three Chopt road, 53

Road from the three Chopt road to the Church, 53

three notchd road, 52

three notch'd road from No. 40 to 46, 53

road in the three notchd road to the Chapple, 52

(road) Treasurer's Runn to the Byrd, 5

road which now goes through Alexander Trents Lowgrounds on Willis's Creek South branch, 51

Road from Tuckahoe to Bollings mill, 19

(road) from the upper Tuckahoe bridge to the County line, 13

road from Tuckahoe Bridge to Woodson's mill Creek, 5

back road over Tuckahoe Creek from the County Line upwards, 5

road from Tuckahoe Creek mill to Hanover County line, 6, 13

road from Tuckahoe Creek mill into the river road towards the Church and fferry, 7, 10

road from Tuckahoe Creek mill to Manakin Town Ferry, 6[(2)]

(road) Tuckahoe Creek to Stony Creek, 5

road from Tye River to ffendlys Gap and to South River, 54

road from Tye River to Waltons ffork of Sclate River and from thence into Glovers road, 47

road from Tye River to Rock fish, 44

road from Thomas Walker's Plantation into Mr. Cary's road, 18

road from Richard Ward's Plantation to his Plantation on Green Creek, 44

Watkins' Path, 26

Road from Watson's Quarter to Collo. Eppes's path, 24

Road from Henry Webb's to the Bird Creek, 28

Road from Webbs' Spring to the Bird Creek, 22

Road from Whitesides's Creek to Woods ffield, 55

road over Willis's Creek, 28

middle road from Willis's River at Albemarl County line, 55

Road from Willis's Creek Bridge to Bear Garden Creek, 33

road from Willis's Bridge to Thompsons branch, 52

road from William Womacks Plantation into Mr. Cary's road, 18

Road from Woods's ffield to the D. S. Tree, 55

Michael Woods road, 41

Road from Joseph Woodson's Path to the County line on South Side of James River, 19

road from Tucker Woodsons fferry into the Mountain road, 44

Signposts, Markers, Direction Stones, etc.:
Direction Stones, 35
D. S. Tree, 41[(3)], 44, 50, 55
Negros Arm, 46
Numbered Trees on the Mountain Ridge Road or Mountain Road. After the Spring of 1743 Old Style this became the Three Notch'd Road.

    Number Twelve, 28, 32, 33
    Number twenty-two, $32^{(2)}$, $33^{(2)}$
    Number twenty six, $33^{(2)}$
    Number Thirty, 28, 32, 33, 43
    Number Thirty Two, 43
    Number thirty six, 32
    Number forty, 30, 53
    Number forty-six, 30, 53
Signposts, 35, 37, 38, 50
Stone on corner of lands of Allen Howard and William Knight, 19

Road Surveyors' Gangs:
John Barnes Gang, 41
Ralph Graves's gang, 46
Mr. Hopkins's Gang, $54^{(2)}$
Anthony Hughes's gang, 48
George Stovals Gang, 41
Wamacks gang, 40

Miscellaneous:
Horn quarter Horse penn, 18
Manacanton low grounds, 11
Manakin (Manacan) Town, 5, $6^{(2)}$, $7^{(2)}$, 12, 14, 15, 16, 17, 25, 29, 31, 38, 40, 46
mount Misery, $23^{(2)}$
The Ordinary, 29
Old Ordinary, 31
the Pit, 5
Alexander Trent's Low grounds, 51

www.ingramcontent.com/pod-product-compliance
Lightning Source LLC
Chambersburg PA
CBHW080742250426
43671CB00038B/2840